The LADIES' VILLAGE
~ IMPROVEMENT ~
SOCIETY COOKBOOK

FLORENCE FABRICANT

The LADIES' VILLAGE IMPROVEMENT SOCIETY COOKBOOK

Eating and Entertaining in East Hampton

PHOTOGRAPHY BY
DOUG YOUNG

FOREWORD BY
MARTHA STEWART

RIZZOLI
NEW YORK

New York · Paris · London · Milan

Dedicated to the many hundreds of women who have volunteered countless hours of hard work, ingenuity, and loving devotion to the community of East Hampton as members of the Ladies' Village Improvement Society.

CONTENTS

FOREWORD

I bought my home on Lily Pond Lane almost thirty years ago. Much has changed in East Hampton since then. Many new houses have been built and countless new stores have opened their doors on Main Street and Newtown Lane. The summer population has swelled, and the beaches have become more crowded.

But some things have remained the same. The giant elm trees that tower over the highway leading into town are still green and stately. The roadsides are still planted with lovely maples and lindens, offering shady avenues and streets on which to walk or bicycle. The scenic village green and its iconic pond, populated by pairs of plump swans, are still the backdrop for many thousands of photographs throughout the year. Wedding parties, family photos, casual selfies, and formal school portraits are still snapped daily in front of the picturesque windmills, too.

The Ladies' Village Improvement Society can claim bragging rights for the glory of this scenery. The LVIS is responsible for the health of those magnificent trees, for the open vista of the long and luxurious village green—as well as the innovative "rain garden" there that helps keep the groundwater pristine—and for inspiring the covenants that protect the architectural integrity of the village's many amazing historic structures. The organization even saw to it that unsightly utility lines were buried underground in the heart of the village.

Like most local and summer residents of East Hampton, I am well aware of the good works of the LVIS over the past century and a quarter. We all love the summer fair, the house and garden tours, and the other community events that raise funds to ensure that the society can continue its efforts. This lovely cookbook, the LVIS's 125th Anniversary Edition—which includes incredible recipes from well-known chefs, famous hostesses, and celebrities, as well as LVIS members—is another way we can support and maintain this beloved institution.

The LVIS is the guardian of the character and beauty of East Hampton, standing strong against the ravages of time and the challenges of a booming population. Our thanks to all the contributors and to our editor, Florence Fabricant, for making this volume an essential addition to everyone's collection of culinary books. I know you will be thrilled with the recipes and will be serving the dishes at your parties and dinners all year long.

Cheers to East Hampton and its traditions,
and brava the LVIS!

MARTHA STEWART

INTRODUCTION

East Hampton beckons in midsummer, when centuries-old trees are in full leaf, roses bedeck rustic fences, the sparkling sea laps the sandy beaches, and farm stands proudly display a kaleidoscope of freshly harvested vegetables and fruits. It draws seasonal visitors who come and then go, eventually leaving bright autumn days, awesomely rough winter surf, and evenings sitting by the fire to those who cherish the region year-round.

Among those, 125 years ago, were some civic-minded residents, all women, who founded the Ladies' Village Improvement Society, or LVIS, to help maintain the character of the village by tending its trees and sidewalks and keeping commercialization at bay. As a vacationer and then a part-time resident, it did not take long for me to appreciate East Hampton's perennial allure.

And as one who cooked, even before the kitchen became my home office, having fresh produce, just-laid eggs, seafood mere hours out of the water, and even some wild treasures like beach plums and blackberries, was irresistible. I discovered nut-sweet bay scallops and heads of ruffled kale in the off-season. I still marvel that I was able to turn all of this into a career.

It really began as a cause. For many consumers back in the 1970s, shopping at farm stands had yet to become the habit it is today, in part because there were fewer of them. Residents and visitors relied on supermarkets for their corn and tomatoes in summer. But I wanted them to know how much better it was to opt for the local harvest. I needed a megaphone! Luckily, Everett Rattray, the editor of the esteemed *East Hampton Star*, saw things my way, was willing to take a chance on an inexperienced journalist, and "In Season" became a regular food column in the weekly newspaper.

Not long after, *The New York Times* came calling, and within six months I became the proud owner of a byline in the *Times*. My gratitude toward East Hampton and all it represents is boundless.

Today the farm stands offer incredible choices—they're even growing wheat out here—and the farmers are thriving now that food lovers, including restaurant chefs, have tuned in to the siren call of a ripe field tomato, corn with husks moist and green, lettuces without wilt, Brussels sprouts on the stalk, unwaxed cucumbers and zucchini, and baskets of berries shipped only a few miles. Healthy farm-to-table fare is what the region has been all about; here it's not just the latest trend.

Treasures from the fields and home gardens, and the wealth of seafood harvested commercially and by amateur surf-casters and clam-diggers, are the backbone of what the area has to offer. In writing this cookbook I have combined my passion for the region's provender with my appreciation for LVIS.

As soon as this project, to mark the 125th anniversary of LVIS, got the green light, members were asked to submit recipes and also the stories that went with them. The cookbook committee joined me in soliciting recipes from some of the marquee figures in the arts and entertainment who also live full- or part-time in the area. LVIS members lit their stoves to lend a much-needed hand in testing the recipes and also in bringing some dishes that appeared in previous LVIS cookbooks up to date.

This is a menu cookbook, arranged seasonally to highlight the local calendar with a supper by the fire in winter, an appreciation of reopened farm stands in spring, strawberry socials, beach picnics, genial cocktail parties, late-season harvests from land and sea after Labor Day, and festive holiday gatherings.

Many of the recipes are enlivened with stories of family traditions, local history, and personal recollections. Baked goods and preserves that LVIS sells at its annual summer fair, dishes from the artist and performer Laurie Anderson, desserts that the actor Alec Baldwin and his wife, Hilaria Baldwin, feed their children, specialties from food celebrities like Martha Stewart and Ina Garten, from the poet Philip Schultz, and even from a notebook belonging to the late painter Lee Krasner, fill this cookbook. There are contributions from restaurants, including Nick & Toni's, Almond, and the 1770 House, from the owners of farm stands and fish markets, from wineries, and from long-time residents like the Daytons, the Rattrays, Devon Fredericks, and members of LVIS.

Most of the dishes for the lunches, dinners, and other events featured in this book keep the seasons in mind. Thus it's a showcase for halibut and bluefish instead of salmon, though if salmon is your preference, by all means use it. If you live down South you might opt for red snapper. This cookbook is not meant as a manifesto but a gentle nudge.

You may be tempted by some specialties that have been part of the culinary fabric of the region for centuries, like rich clam pies and chowders, beach plum preserves, and the local take on grits.

The menus also suggest what to drink. Again I've stressed local because since 1973 the area has become a flourishing wine region. It's mainly on the North Fork reached by road or ferry, but also on the South Fork, where rows of leafy vineyards have replaced potatoes and cauliflower grown for the wholesale market. There are now around fifty wineries on Eastern Long Island, an area with weather tempered by the sea, as it is in Bordeaux.

White, red, and sparkling wines, along with beer and cider, also made locally, are suggested for the menus. You may not have access to what is grown here, but you still might find drinks made in your locality or from elsewhere across the globe to complement these menus. Members of LVIS and East End bartenders have also shared their cocktail recipes.

From start to finish, this cookbook is a celebration. It's a fanfare for LVIS and its members marking 125 years of fruitful good work, and also for the region, its history, traditions, and honest, good food.

—FLORENCE FABRICANT

IMPROVEMENTS: Most of the recipes include an "improvement," meant as a play on the name of the organization but also to convey a tip, another use, or a variation that can enhance the recipe.

The Ladies' Village Improvement Society: Who We Are

The world of the Ladies' Village Improvement Society of East Hampton is a world of abundance—of lemonade mornings when children rush to be the first through the gate of Playland at the annual summer fair; of wide-porch afternoons whiled away in old wicker chairs as the light turns mellow-gold and the very last brownie is secretly devoured in solitude. Of the good earth—the South Fork's warm, fine loam that produces the world's best potatoes and corn. Of the endlessly rolling ocean waves into which the tourists and the townspeople plunge, as the sun sparkles and, unseen but close by, the striped bass and the bluefish swim in swirling schools.

Page 16: The stalwart cookbook committee of the LVIS posed on July 6, 1948, shortly before that year's cookbook publication.

WHAT IS THE LADIES' VILLAGE IMPROVEMENT SOCIETY?

In simplest terms, it is a volunteer organization, founded in 1895 and dedicated to preserving the beauty of the Village of East Hampton. In more fanciful terms, the LVIS is the heart and soul of a very old American town. Or, some might say, a sort of shadow government of good-doing women, who plan and organize and grease the wheels of civic improvement in this storied village of green lawns and blue hydrangeas.

In some ways, the LVIS is all the things that its antiquated name seems to suggest: yes, it is a women's organization; yes, the women are known to wear straw hats and aprons; yes, some of these women make beach plum jelly.

But, as in almost everything, the preconceived notions don't even begin to reveal the deeper story. Alongside the Relief Society and the Young Women's Christian Association, the LVIS is one of the oldest continually running women's organizations in the United States.

The LVIS may begin with the genteel word lady—a word that has fallen into disuse, if not outright disrepute—but make no mistake about it: the LVIS is mighty.

The nearly 300 members of the LVIS are celebrating its 125th anniversary in 2020, but the idea of starting something like it actually dates back a few years more.

Yellowed news clippings from the archives of *The East Hampton Star* tell the origin story.

In February of 1891—February being then, as now, the quietest month on the South Fork, a month when grand plans are dreamed up and plots hatched—an unnamed resident who signed him- or herself simply "Citizen" wrote a letter to Mr. Boughton, the editor of the *Star*, announcing his or her intention to create an improvement society that would grapple with the miserable state of the roads and the lack of drainage along Main Street. This energetic correspondent—suspicion falls on Ellen Hedges, who would become the group's first president—wrote again in September of that year, agitating for action to keep down dust on the streets.

At that time, village improvement societies were, as they say, a thing. There were groups active all over Long Island, in Riverhead,

Left: A rare glass-plate image of Clinton Academy, a boys' school dating back to colonial days that lives on as a community gathering place and museum, as seen in the 1890s, around the time the LVIS held its first meeting there to discuss improvements of the roads (alternately mired in mud or too dusty) and the sidewalks (almost nonexistent).

Below: The Gardiner "Brown" House, built in 1747, is now the headquarters of the LVIS—and only a very short stroll up Main Street from Clinton Academy. It houses meeting rooms, offices, and the beloved second-hand shops (filled with furniture, housewares, books, and clothes) that are a major source of financial sustenance for the nonprofit organization's many good works, from tree care to scholarships.

Dancing at the LVIS Fair, July 1915. The annual fête was held first on the Town Green (as here), then for decades at historic Mulford Farm, and lately at the Gardiner "Brown" House. Foxtrots no longer figure in the festivities, but some traditions, from the children's Playland to the silent auction, are perennial.

Mattituck, Southampton, and Orient. Typically, their campaigns tackled public-nuisance and health-and-safety problems that might be fixed by the installation of proper sidewalks, or electric street lights, or curbs to separate fetid street runoff from the dainty kid boots of the pedestrian.

Mr. Boughton seems to have been in cahoots with whoever this Citizen was: he regularly published editorials with titles like "What Women of Port Jefferson Have Done" and "What Sag Harbor Ladies Have Done" as a challenge to East Hampton.

Finally, on November 29, 1895, a call went out inviting interested women to attend a meeting in the annex of Clinton Academy. Some twenty-one convened that evening. By December, the newly formed "Ladies' Village Improvement Society of East Hampton" was throwing its first fundraising effort: a "New England supper" on a Tuesday evening, costing twenty-five cents a head.

The emblem of the LVIS is an elm tree in leafy glory. This is because one of the most significant achievements of its volunteer corps is to plant, protect, and nurture the shade trees that line the village's main thoroughfares.

The elm was once so ubiquitous it could be called the all-American tree—hence, the presence of an Elm Street in small towns from coast to coast—but since the 1950s, they have been

largely wiped out across the country by Dutch elm disease. Not so here: the elms under the care of the LVIS, which currently tends 114 of them, as well as thousands of other shade species, have been remarkably resilient. What would East Hampton be without the green branches that reach across Woods Lane to create a high triumphal arch at the entrance to the village?

Even if all the LVIS had done was protect East Hampton's trees, it would have been remarkable. But these strong, active—sometimes even visionary—women did so much more.

They did, indeed, buy water carts to sprinkle the streets and keep the dust down. Soon they were repairing rickety fences and improving sidewalks so bicyclists could ride without being thrown into the roadside ditch. They twisted the power company's arm to have power lines buried, and waded into the muddy problem of Town Pond—saving it from being drained and filled and then hiring crews to make a proper pond out of what had been a stagnant, marshy, unsightly sink. They got creative with decorative shrubbery to conceal the ugly new Long Island Rail Road embankment.

In the 1920s, the ladies wrestled local real estate agents and merchants to the mat, convincing them that commercial signage was an eyesore, and that eyesores weren't good for business. They won the cooperation of 100 percent of the businessmen, and in 1926 declared East Hampton to be America's "first signless town." (It is no longer signless, alas, but billboards are still kept at bay.)

A float in a 1936 parade broadcast the LVIS's longtime motto, "Keep East Hampton Beautiful." Beautification efforts weren't just about planting shrubs to hide a railway embankment or agitating for the banning of billboards or the burial of power lines, but also about the preservation of the town's priceless built heritage.

In 1954, they gave out their first scholarship to a college-bound East Hampton High School student (and today give out some $150,000 each year).

In the early 1970s, a group of LVIS women from the landmarks committee realized that historical structures in the village were under threat. An intrepid team rolled up their sleeves and kicked off the movement that eventually resulted in the creation of the Main Street Historic District, which has preserved for posterity our most-photographed postcard views, including the iconic windmills under which we so often see daytrippers and wedding parties posing. In 1980, the LVIS conducted an "architectural inventory" of all the village's historic buildings, spurring the creation of further historic districts. And in 1982, it published a book on the subject that brought national attention to the grand old Shingle-style houses of the summer colony. Through these actions, the ladies were the bulwark that stood between our built heritage and the wrecking ball. This was not easy work.

Meanwhile, they have: Fed the ducks at the Nature Trail for sixty-five winters and counting. Sold pencils to buy sapling trees. Cleaned up garbage dumped alongside the ancient wood-cutting paths in Northwest Woods. Hosted Easter dances and New Year's dances and square dances. Compiled and sold thirteen cookbooks, including this one—dating back to the first, in 1896. Planted honeysuckles in front of Town Hall.

It is striking to note that the stated intention of the LVIS was not to change the character or landscape of East Hampton, but to preserve all its timeworn charm and, to borrow an early member's word, its "ruralness."

Reading through old accounts, and sorting through old photographs, it is also striking what an intriguing omnium gatherum of women have been members. This wasn't just a straw-hat-and-white-wicker organization for the hometown elites and those summer residents who lived along Lily Pond Lane and spent their days on the tennis courts at the Maidstone Club—although it was also that. Its membership did then, and still does, cut across social boundaries.

From the start, the toniest crowd pitched in, taking off their white gloves and putting on work gloves to hammer together a broken arbor. Here, we glimpse young Bouviers and Beales in the back seat of a touring car festooned with roses for a parade. There, we see the middle school science teacher dressed as a Dutch maid to serve tea at the refreshment booth at the fair.

John Drew, the world-famous thespian—a much-admired summer resident and member of East Hampton's volunteer fire brigade—posed with the family of John V. Bouvier Jr. at the LVIS Fair (including Jacqueline Bouvier Kennedy's father, young "Black Jack"), c. 1916.

What makes this all so pleasing is that the range of women among the LVIS numbers, down the years, has reflected the diversity of the town itself. Although it must be mentioned that it wasn't until the last three or four decades that women of color have joined, the ranks for a long time now have been drawn from the various ethnic, economic, and religious backgrounds.

The LVIS is Abstract Expressionist painters and golf pros and actresses and heiresses and doctors and executives and stay-at-home moms, physical therapists, shopkeepers, birders, needlepoint experts, historians, hairdressers.

This is a group of powerful women, expressing their power in practical ways, and they changed the future course of our town.

The LVIS has always been nonpolitical—or apolitical, if you prefer—but that doesn't mean the challenges tackled weren't, sometimes, very hard or really quite serious.

The ladies have steered their ship straight and true for 125 years, through the Great Depression, two world wars, the subcultural upheavals of the 1960s, and the Great Recession.

Our community is more than a cliché. We aren't just mansions and movie stars, privet hedges and hedge-fund managers. We earn our livings fishing, farming, teaching stand-up-paddleboarding, running day-care centers, selling skateboards, driving fuel-oil trucks, writing novels, designing nightgowns . . .

It is this multiplicity, this bounty—the abundance not just of the farm stand and the saltwater harvest, but of the culture of the East End—that we celebrate with this cookbook.

—BESS RATTRAY

Clockwise from top left: Young ladies of East Hampton on Main Street at the turn of the twentieth century (when it was visibly in need of civic improvement). Picnicking on Montauk, 1890s. The LVIS Fair committee, 1940s. Dressed as Dutch maids to sell tea at the 1934 fair. The LVIS softball team, 1950s. At the baked goods booth during the 2019 fair. Members attend a tournament at the Maidstone Club, 1950s. A fundraising tea at Guild Hall, 1920s.

SCALLIONS
$1 each

OUR
EGGPLANT
$2.50
/lb

OUR
PARSLEY
$2.50 each

OUR
ZUCCHINI
$2.50

OUR RED PEPPERS
$3.50/lb

OUR
RADISHES

OUR
ARUGULA
2.50

The LADIES' VILLAGE
~ IMPROVEMENT ~
SOCIETY COOKBOOK

The FARM STANDS REOPEN

Timing is everything. It's often May before the farm stands have anything to sell, and by that time, cooks have been yearning for overflowing baskets of fresh produce. The oceanic climate drives the arrival of springtime weather late, but when the seas do finally warm, they keep the growing season going well into fall. In spring, green stuff comes first: asparagus, spinach, and herbs; and then later radishes. Soon there will be peas and cucumbers, but not soon enough. This menu reflects what can be done in spring, as the farms begin to kick into high gear. Is it too soon to break open that bottle of rosé? Probably not.

Fettuccine with Asparagus and Blue Cheese
Spinach and Endive Salad • Perfection Pork Chops
Bittersweet Chocolate Pound Cake

Fettuccine with Asparagus and Blue Cheese

PIERRE FRANEY

1¼ POUNDS MEDIUM ASPARAGUS, ENDS SNAPPED OFF

2 TABLESPOONS EXTRA VIRGIN OLIVE OIL

2 TABLESPOONS UNSALTED BUTTER

4 WELL-DRAINED CANNED PLUM TOMATOES, SEEDED AND DICED

1 CLOVE GARLIC, MINCED

SALT

12 OUNCES FETTUCCINE

FRESHLY GROUND BLACK PEPPER

4 OUNCES AMERICAN BLUE CHEESE, CRUMBLED

¼ CUP COARSELY CHOPPED FLAT-LEAF PARSLEY LEAVES

FRESHLY GRATED PARMIGIANO-REGGIANO FOR SERVING

Slice the asparagus on the bias into ½-inch pieces.

Heat the olive oil and butter in a large skillet over medium heat. Add the asparagus, tomatoes, and garlic and sauté, stirring, for about 2 minutes, until the asparagus becomes somewhat tender. Remove from the heat. This step can be completed up to an hour in advance.

Shortly before serving, bring a large pot of salted water to a boil and add the fettuccine. Cook until al dente, 6 to 7 minutes. Remove ½ cup of the pasta water and reserve. Drain the fettuccine and add it to the skillet with the asparagus. Season with pepper. Heat over medium-low, using tongs to incorporate the ingredients. Add half the reserved pasta water and the blue cheese. Stir to combine the ingredients, adding more pasta water as needed. Season with more salt and pepper if desired, shower with the parsley, and serve with the Parmigiano-Reggiano on the side.

IMPROVEMENT: Feta cheese can be a nice stand-in for the blue cheese.

This French chef settled in Springs and lived in the town for decades. His son, Jacques, owns a wine shop in town. Pierre Franey was also known as Craig Claiborne's cooking partner at *The New York Times*. The two of them wrote countless columns in Claiborne's house, Franey at the stove and Claiborne typing away, trying to keep up. "How many cups was that, Pierre?" he would call out. Though he was French through and through, American food rubbed off on Franey, as with this recipe, which is not particularly French at all.

SERVES 4

Spinach is an early crop from local farms. This salad, easily assembled, combines spinach with endive, not local but available to enliven greens in early spring.

SERVES 4

IMPROVEMENTS: This salad is something of a blank slate. Other ingredients, like sautéed mushrooms, bacon, cucumbers, slivered prosciutto, and chopped hard-boiled egg, can be added.

Spinach and Endive Salad
FLORENCE FABRICANT

12 OUNCES BABY SPINACH, TORN

2 ENDIVES, QUARTERED LENGTHWISE, CORES REMOVED, SLIVERED ON AN ANGLE

4 TABLESPOONS EXTRA VIRGIN OLIVE OIL

1 CUP THINLY SLICED RED ONION

1 TABLESPOON DIJON MUSTARD

2 TABLESPOONS RED WINE VINEGAR

SALT AND FRESHLY GROUND BLACK PEPPER

½ CUP COARSELY CHOPPED PECANS

Place the spinach and endives in a salad bowl and toss.

Heat the oil in a medium skillet over medium heat, add the onion, and sauté until it is translucent and just beginning to color, 2 to 3 minutes. Stir in the mustard. Remove from the heat and add the vinegar. Stir. Pour the dressing and onions over the spinach and endives and toss. Season with salt and pepper, scatter the pecans on top, and serve.

Perfection Pork Chops

BONNY REIFF-SMITH

4 BONELESS PORK LOIN CHOPS, ABOUT 1 INCH THICK OR
    SLIGHTLY MORE, PREFERABLY HERITAGE BREED

1 TEASPOON CHINESE FIVE-SPICE POWDER

½ CUP SOY SAUCE

¼ CUP KETCHUP OR GOCHUJANG (KOREAN "KETCHUP")

¼ CUP TOASTED SESAME OIL

1 MEDIUM ONION, MINCED

4 CLOVES GARLIC, MINCED

1½ TEASPOONS MINCED FRESH GINGER

FRESH CILANTRO FOR GARNISH

Rub the pork chops with the five-spice powder.

In a small bowl, mix together the soy sauce, ketchup, sesame oil, onion, garlic, and ginger. Reserve half this mixture and refrigerate it. Place the rest in a large sealable plastic bag or a dish with cover that's large enough to hold the pork chops. Add the pork chops and turn them in the marinade until they are well coated. Cover, refrigerate, and let marinate for at least 8 hours or overnight.

Heat a grill or broiler and cook the pork chops for 8 to 10 minutes on each side for medium. An instant-read thermometer should register 145°F. Remove the chops to a platter and tent with foil. Let rest for 10 minutes. Bring the reserved marinade mixture to a simmer and transfer to a bowl to serve alongside the chops. Garnish the chops with cilantro and serve.

IMPROVEMENTS: You can slice the chops about ½ inch thick, arrange them on a platter, and drizzle the sauce on top. Or you could toss 6 ounces of udon or soba noodles, cooked, with the sauce and arrange on a platter with the sliced pork on top.

The secret, according to this LVIS and cookbook committee member and accomplished cook, is to let the pork chops marinate overnight. And do not overcook them. Korean gochujang, a spicy ketchup-style condiment, is increasingly available, even in supermarkets.

SERVES 4

This recipe from a restaurant once known as the Laundry comes via the food editor for *The East Hampton Star*, who worked in the restaurant's kitchen. The Laundry was established in 1980 in a former commercial laundry building—long before the famous chef Thomas Keller opened his French Laundry in a recycled laundry building in Yountville, California. Leif Hope, the owner, opened the East Hampton restaurant thanks to a lengthy list of backers, many of whom were in show business and the arts, a precious guarantee that they would be able to book a table.

The illustrious place, which closed in its original location decades ago, was designed by the award-winning architect Norman Jaffe, a Bridgehampton resident. It is now occupied by Dopo La Spiaggia (see recipe, page 54).

SERVES 12

IMPROVEMENT: Icing on the cake? Consider the chocolate glaze used on Nana's Rum-Laced Brownies (page 108).

Bittersweet Chocolate Pound Cake
LAURA DONNELLY, ORIGINAL LAUNDRY RESTAURANT

8 OUNCES (2 STICKS) UNSALTED BUTTER, SOFTENED

2 CUPS PLUS 2 TABLESPOONS GRANULATED SUGAR

1½ CUPS ALL-PURPOSE FLOUR

¾ CUP UNSWEETENED COCOA POWDER

¾ TEASPOON BAKING POWDER

½ TEASPOON BAKING SODA

½ TEASPOON SALT

1½ TEASPOONS INSTANT COFFEE POWDER

3 LARGE EGGS

1½ TEASPOONS VANILLA EXTRACT

¾ CUP BUTTERMILK, OR ½ CUP PLAIN YOGURT DISSOLVED IN ¼ CUP WATER

SIFTED CONFECTIONERS' SUGAR FOR DUSTING

FRESH STRAWBERRIES FOR SERVING

Preheat the oven to 325°F. Brush a 9 by 5 by 3-inch loaf pan with 1 tablespoon of the butter and dust with 2 tablespoons of the granulated sugar. Shake off any excess.

Whisk together the flour, cocoa powder, baking powder, baking soda, salt, and coffee powder in a large bowl. Place the remaining butter in the bowl of a stand mixer and beat until creamy. Add the remaining 2 cups granulated sugar and beat until light and fluffy. Scrape down the sides of the bowl. Beat in the eggs one at a time until well blended. Beat in the vanilla. Add the flour mixture in three portions alternately with the buttermilk. Beat on low speed just until smooth.

Spoon into the prepared pan and bake for about 1 hour, or slightly longer, until fairly firm yet still springy on the surface and a cake tester comes out clean. Place on a rack and cool to room temperature. Unmold and serve on a platter dusted with confectioners' sugar and surrounded by strawberries.

STRAWBERRY TIME

East End strawberries are a treasure. They perfume the fields as they ripen; quart-size baskets of them add fragrance to farm stands. There was a time when strawberry socials open to the public were commonplace in the area; they're a rarity now. Today, far fewer farms open their strawberry fields to the public for pick-your-own. If you can find one, go picking, and bring children—picking is not backbreaking work for them. I adore the memories of my children, happily rewarded with their own overflowing baskets, their fingers, faces, and clothing stained red.

Even without venturing into the fields I rarely buy strawberries unless they are locally grown, which means that I only serve strawberries from late May to mid-July. The local berries allowed to ripen on the vine are richer and juicier than others. Note that strawberries are among the most heavily treated crops of all; local farmers go much lighter on the chemicals than growers whose berries require long-distance shipping.

Strawberry Rhubarb Pie • Victoria Sandwich
Strawberry Shortcakes

Strawberry Rhubarb Pie
LOAVES & FISHES

PASTRY (RECIPE FOLLOWS)

3 CUPS HULLED AND HALVED FRESH STRAWBERRIES

4 CUPS (3 TO 4 STALKS) SLICED FRESH RHUBARB (½-INCH SLICES)

1⅓ CUPS SUGAR

½ TEASPOON GROUND CINNAMON

¼ CUP CORNSTARCH

1 LARGE EGG YOLK

1 TABLESPOON HEAVY CREAM

WHIPPED CREAM, CRÈME FRAÎCHE, OR ICE CREAM FOR SERVING

Prepare the pastry.

Preheat the oven to 350°F.

Combine the strawberries and rhubarb in a large bowl. Add all but 2 tablespoons of the sugar, the cinnamon, and cornstarch. Toss the ingredients together until well blended. Set aside.

Divide the pastry dough into two slightly uneven portions. Roll the larger piece into a 12-inch circle. Set into a 9-inch pie plate, preferably glass. Pile the strawberry filling into the pie plate. Roll the rest of the dough into a circle and place it over the filling. Seal and crimp the edges. Use a sharp paring knife or scissors to cut a few decorative slits in the top crust. As an alternative, the pastry for the top crust can be cut in strips and woven into a lattice.

Whisk the egg yolk and cream in a small bowl and brush on the top crust. Sprinkle with the remaining 2 tablespoons sugar. Place in the oven and bake for 50 minutes to 1 hour, until the pastry is nicely browned. Remove from the oven and allow to cool for at least 1 hour. Serve with whipped cream, crème fraîche, or ice cream.

IMPROVEMENT: Rinse and then refrigerate fresh strawberries with their hulls intact. They will hold up better that way. Hull them just before you use them.

The small white store just off Montauk Highway at the Sagaponack stoplight has been a fine food destination for decades, famous for high quality and Rolls-Royce prices that do not deter its carriage-trade clientele. This straightforward rendition of the seasonal combination of strawberries and rhubarb is a delicious confection from its kitchen, a recipe by Anna Pump, whose daughter, Sybille van Kempen, now runs the store.

SERVES 8

PASTRY

MAKES A TWO-CRUST PASTRY FOR A 9-INCH PIE

2 CUPS ALL-PURPOSE FLOUR, PLUS MORE FOR ROLLING

2 TABLESPOONS SUGAR

½ TEASPOON SALT

8 OUNCES (2 STICKS) COLD UNSALTED BUTTER, CUT INTO SMALL PIECES

1 TABLESPOON LEMON JUICE

⅓ CUP ICE WATER

Place the flour, sugar, and salt in a food processor. Pulse briefly to combine. Add the butter and pulse until the mixture is uniformly crumbly. Combine the lemon juice with the ice water. Pour about half this mixture into the work bowl and pulse briefly. Add the remaining water mixture and pulse a few times, until the dough begins to come together. If needed, add a little more water. Gather the dough into a ball, flatten it, wrap it in plastic, and refrigerate for 30 minutes

Victoria Sandwich

IAN SCOLLAY, MAIDSTONE CLUB

4 OUNCES (1 STICK) UNSALTED BUTTER, SOFTENED, PLUS MORE FOR THE PAN

2 CUPS ALL-PURPOSE FLOUR

2 TEASPOONS BAKING POWDER

½ TEASPOON SALT

1 CUP GRANULATED SUGAR

3 LARGE EGGS

1 TEASPOON VANILLA EXTRACT

⅔ CUP WHOLE MILK

1½ CUPS HEAVY CREAM

½ CUP CRÈME FRAÎCHE

1 CUP STRAWBERRY PRESERVES, PREFERABLY LOCALLY MADE

CONFECTIONERS' SUGAR FOR DUSTING

FRESH STRAWBERRIES FOR GARNISH

Preheat the oven to 300°F. Butter an 8-inch springform pan and line the bottom with parchment.

Whisk together the flour, baking powder, and salt in a medium bowl. Set aside.

Place the butter in the bowl of a mixer and beat on medium until creamy. Add the granulated sugar and beat until light and fluffy, about 5 minutes. Beat in the eggs, one at a time, until well blended. Beat in the vanilla. Add half the flour mixture, then half the milk and beat just enough to combine. Repeat with the remaining flour mixture and milk. Pour the batter into the prepared pan and smooth the top.

Bake for about 1 hour, until the cake is golden brown, begins to shrink from the sides of the pan, and a cake tester comes out clean. Remove to a wire rack and allow to cool completely.

Slice the cake in half horizontally. Whip the cream with the crème fraîche until not quite stiff. Spread the strawberry preserves over the bottom layer of the cake, spread whipped cream over the preserves, and then sandwich with the top layer. Dust with confectioners' sugar. Serve immediately, or refrigerate, uncovered, until ready to serve. Decorate with fresh strawberries.

The Maidstone Club is an imposing and venerable Tudor-style beachfront presence, often shrouded in mist. The chef there, Ian Scollay, has reinterpreted an English teatime favorite. His is made with a rich pound cake, not a sponge cake like the original, named for Queen Victoria in the mid-nineteenth century. The Victoria Sandwich soon became popular across the pond, and then in the United States; a recipe appeared in Isabella Beeton's cookbook in 1874. It was long believed that some of East Hampton's first settlers came from Maidstone, a town southwest of London; this is why many local places bear the name.

SERVES 12

IMPROVEMENT: Using great care, you can divide the cake into three layers for a truly exceptional dessert.

First strawberries, then peas. And on to leafy greens, cucumbers, other berries, and bouquets of flowers. And soon come the much-anticipated tomatoes, first from Riverhead, then marked "our own." And corn, among the best in the region, which will be available into early fall along with peaches, potatoes, apples, and stalks of Brussels sprouts. And thus Pike's marks the season. The rustic, unpretentious stand, hardly more than a couple of lean-tos overlooking the fields with a hand-painted sign, is a magnet for cooks.

SERVES 12

IMPROVEMENT: Adding some crème fraîche to the heavy cream as you whip it will help stabilize the whipped cream so it will hold for hours, even overnight, without breaking down.

Strawberry Shortcakes
JENNIFER PIKE, PIKE FARMS

1 TABLESPOON UNSALTED BUTTER, SOFTENED, FOR THE PAN

2¼ CUPS ALL-PURPOSE FLOUR

1 TABLESPOON BAKING POWDER

½ TEASPOON BAKING SODA

1 TABLESPOON SUGAR, PLUS MORE FOR THE BERRIES

1 TEASPOON SALT

4 TABLESPOONS COLD UNSALTED BUTTER, CUT INTO SMALL PIECES

1½ CUPS COLD BUTTERMILK

2 QUARTS LOCAL STRAWBERRIES, HULLED AND HALVED

2 CUPS HEAVY CREAM

½ CUP CRÈME FRAÎCHE

Preheat the oven to 500°F. Butter a 9-inch round cake pan, preferably with a loose bottom, with the softened butter.

Whisk together the flour, baking powder, baking soda, sugar, and salt in a medium bowl. Add the cold butter, pinching it in with your fingertips or using a pastry blender or fork, until the mixture is uniformly mealy. Add the buttermilk and stir to combine. The dough will be quite wet.

Drop blobs of the dough in the pan in about 12 portions, 9 around the outside and 3 in the middle. Place in the oven and bake for 5 minutes. Reduce the oven temperature to 425°F and bake until the biscuits are golden brown, about 15 minutes longer.

Cool in the pan for about 2 minutes. Run a knife around the edges, remove the entire set of biscuits from the pan, and place on a rack, right side up. (If you are using a pan with a loose bottom, remove the sides of the pan and place the biscuits on the rack.)

Place the strawberries in a bowl and add sugar to taste. Whip the cream with the crème fraîche in a mixing bowl until it holds peaks.

When the biscuits have cooled, separate them and split each in half. Place the bottom halves on plates or a serving platter, top with strawberries and whipped cream, replace the tops of the biscuits, and serve, or refrigerate until ready to serve.

LUNCH AROUND *the* POOL

Though pools are in good supply throughout the
community, one is not required for enjoying this
lunch. But an al fresco setting–a porch, a deck,
a lawn, and a balmy day–would be ideal.
The components could even be transported,
well wrapped and in a cooler, to a beach or
pond-side location. The menu is elegant, exploits
summer's bounty, and offers the advantage of being
assembled from recipes that can all be made well
in advance. Everything can be expanded to serve
more guests. Lemonade, iced tea, or summer's
inevitable pink wine from a South Fork vineyard
will suit this menu.

Melon Gazpacho • Lobster Cakes
Zucchini, Feta, and Olive Slaw • Blueberry Buckle

The ease with which this recipe is made is almost magical. The flavor shines without even a drop of the usual lemon or lime juice that typically enhances ripe melon. But when the creator is chef Eric Ripert, a Sag Harbor resident and the co-owner of Le Bernardin in New York, a restaurant at the pinnacle of the ratings scale, this achievement comes as no surprise.

SERVES 6

Melon Gazpacho
ERIC RIPERT

1 RIPE MEDIUM-LARGE CANTALOUPE OR LOCAL MUSK MELON, PEELED, SEEDED, AND ROUGHLY CHOPPED

3 CUPS ICE CUBES

1 TABLESPOON FINE SEA SALT, OR TO TASTE

GENEROUS PINCH OF GROUND WHITE PEPPER

½ CUP HIGH-QUALITY EXTRA VIRGIN OLIVE OIL

6 SMALL SPRIGS BASIL

Place the melon in a food processor and puree. Transfer to a blender and blend with the ice, salt, and pepper until smooth and frothy. (If you have a heavy-duty blender like a Vitamix, you can blend the ingredients directly, without using the food processor first for the melon.) You may have to do the pureeing in two shifts, depending on the capacity of your machines. Slowly drizzle in the olive oil with the machine running.

Transfer to a large bowl or container, cover, and refrigerate for at least 1 hour or up to 2 days. To serve, check the seasoning, transfer to bowls, mugs, or glasses, and top with the basil.

IMPROVEMENT: Refrigerate the bowls or mugs for a few hours in advance; serving the soup in chilled containers will help keep it cool.

Lobster Cakes
CHARLOTTE SASSO, STUART'S SEAFOOD MARKET

3½ TABLESPOONS UNSALTED BUTTER

3 SCALLIONS, TRIMMED AND FINELY CHOPPED

1 LARGE CLOVE GARLIC, MINCED

1 POUND COOKED FRESH LOBSTER MEAT, CUT INTO ½-INCH DICE

1 TABLESPOON MINCED FLAT-LEAF PARSLEY

1 TEASPOON DIJON MUSTARD

⅔ CUP MAYONNAISE

1 LARGE EGG, BEATEN

DASH OF HOT SAUCE

SALT AND FRESHLY GROUND BLACK PEPPER

1¼ CUPS PANKO BREAD CRUMBS

6 LEMON WEDGES FOR SERVING

TARTAR SAUCE, RUSSIAN DRESSING, OR YUZU-LEMON AIOLI (OPTIONAL) FOR SERVING (SEE YUZU-LEMON AIOLI, PAGE 89)

Melt 1 tablespoon of the butter in a medium skillet over medium-low heat. Add the scallions and garlic and cook until softened and barely starting to brown, about 3 minutes. Add the lobster and parsley, stir, and sauté briefly, just enough to combine the ingredients. Transfer to a medium bowl.

Fold in the mustard, mayonnaise, egg, and hot sauce and season with salt and pepper. Fold in ¾ cup of the panko. Refrigerate for at least 30 minutes or up to 3 hours.

Shape into 6 cakes. Coat each with the remaining panko. Heat the remaining 2½ tablespoons butter in the skillet over medium heat. Cook the lobster cakes for about 3 minutes per side, until golden and cooked through. Serve with lemon wedges and your choice of sauce, if using.

IMPROVEMENT: For a pound of lobster meat you will need about four 1¼-pound lobsters. Other seafood, like crabmeat, chopped sea scallops, diced cooked monkfish, salmon, shrimp, or a mixture, can replace the lobster.

Back in the day the lobsters were local. That is rarely true these days, due to climate change and warming seas. Still, lobster is abundant on Hamptons menus as a perennial summertime favorite. Stuart's Seafood in Amagansett has long been one of the area's most venerable and reliable markets.

SERVES 6

Art of Eating is one of the best-known caterers in the area. This salad, like the melon gazpacho on this menu, is dressed without vinegar or other acid; the dish does not need it. The feta cheese marvelously punches up the flavor.

SERVES 6

Zucchini, Feta, and Olive Slaw
CHERYL STAIR, ART OF EATING

3 SMALL GREEN ZUCCHINI, TRIMMED AND JULIENNED

3 SMALL GOLDEN ZUCCHINI, TRIMMED AND JULIENNED

1 MEDIUM RIPE TOMATO, PEELED, CORED, AND FINELY DICED

2 SCALLIONS, THINLY SLICED ON A SLANT

2 CLOVES GARLIC, MINCED

4 OUNCES FETA CHEESE, DICED

10 KALAMATA OLIVES, PITTED AND COARSELY CHOPPED

8 FRESH BASIL LEAVES, TORN INTO BITS

SALT AND FRESHLY GROUND BLACK PEPPER

3 TABLESPOONS EXTRA VIRGIN OLIVE OIL

Toss the zucchini, tomato, scallions, and garlic together in a salad bowl. Fold in the cheese, olives, and basil. Season with salt and pepper. Fold in the olive oil.

Set aside to marinate for 30 minutes, fold the ingredients together again, and serve.

IMPROVEMENT: Another firm, salty cheese, like ricotta salata or Roquefort, can be used in place of the feta.

The LVIS member who contributed this recipe likes to call it "unbuckle" for what it threatens to do to the waistline. Buckles, slumps, duffs, cobblers, and the like represent a category of old-fashioned baked fruit desserts. This one takes advantage of the abundant blueberry crop that goes from midsummer into fall.

SERVES 6 TO 10

Blueberry Buckle
ABIGAIL VOGEL

8 OUNCES (2 STICKS) UNSALTED BUTTER
2⅓ CUPS ALL-PURPOSE FLOUR
½ TEASPOON SALT
2 TEASPOONS BAKING POWDER
¾ CUP PACKED DARK BROWN SUGAR
½ TEASPOON GROUND CINNAMON
1 LARGE EGG, AT ROOM TEMPERATURE
½ CUP GRANULATED SUGAR
½ CUP WHOLE MILK
2½ CUPS FRESH BLUEBERRIES
WHIPPED CREAM, CRÈME FRAÎCHE, OR ICE CREAM FOR SERVING

Preheat the oven to 350°F.

Melt 1 stick of the butter and use a little of it to grease a 3-quart baking dish. Whisk together 2 cups of the flour, the salt, and baking powder in a small bowl. Set aside. Mix the remaining ⅓ cup flour with ½ cup of the brown sugar and the cinnamon in another small bowl. Dice the remaining stick of butter, add it to the brown sugar mixture, and use a pastry blender, your fingertips, or a fork to mix the ingredients until crumbly. Set aside.

Beat the egg in a large bowl by hand or with an electric mixer. Beat in the granulated sugar until thick and light. Beat in the remaining ¼ cup dark brown sugar. Stir in the milk alternately with the flour mixture. Fold in the blueberries. Spoon the mixture into the prepared baking dish and strew with the crumb mixture.

Bake until lightly browned on top and a cake tester comes out clean, about 45 minutes. Allow to cool for at least 1 hour. Serve with whipped cream, crème fraîche, or ice cream.

IMPROVEMENT: For a more wholesome dessert, consider using some or all whole wheat flour in place of the white flour.

PASTA on the PORCH

Dining outdoors on a soft summer evening is a
joy. This al fresco dinner is suitable to serve on
a porch, a deck, or at tables on a lawn, especially
before the end of July when the light doesn't fade
until midevening. But it could also be graced
by a candlelit setting. The notion of offering
two complementary pasta dishes seasoned with
summer's bright tomatoes and fragrant herbs is
innovative and fun. The main course calls for
grilling but can be fully cooked shortly before
guests arrive and served at room temperature.
Dessert can be prepared in advance. Select a light
red wine, like a young merlot, to sip alongside.

Trofie al Pesto • Pasta with Uncooked Tomato Sauce
Butterflied Leg of Lamb • Rainbow Peppers
Blackberries with Barbados Cream

There's basil galore sold at farm stands or picked from backyards and even flowerpots on a deck. Pesto made from local basil is sold at most of the stands, from Amber Waves and Round Swamp Farm to the Green Thumb. But the important feature of this recipe, which was contributed by a chef whose Italian seafood restaurant now occupies the former Laundry restaurant building (see page 34), is quickly blanching then icing the basil. That's what you must do if you want your pesto to remain bright green. Try to find basil with smaller leaves; it will have the best flavor.

SERVES 4

IMPROVEMENT: This recipe includes potatoes with the pasta, a typical recipe from Liguria, the coastal region of Northern Italy that is the home of pesto. Some recipes also include inch-long pieces of tender cooked green beans. You can add those, too.

Trofie al Pesto

MAURIZIO MARFOGLIA, DOPO LA SPIAGGIA

BASIL PESTO (RECIPE FOLLOWS)

SALT

4 MEDIUM RED BLISS POTATOES (ABOUT 8 OUNCES), CUT INTO ¾-INCH DICE

1 POUND TROFIE OR OTHER SHORT TWISTED PASTA (SUCH AS STROZZAPRETI, FUSILLI, OR GEMELLI)

GRATED PARMIGIANO-REGGIANO FOR SERVING

Prepare the basil pesto.

Bring a large pot of salted water to a boil. Add the potatoes and pasta and cook for about 10 minutes, until the pasta is al dente. Remove ½ cup of the pasta water to a large, warm bowl. Stir the pesto sauce into the water. Drain the pasta and potatoes, add to the bowl, fold the ingredients together, and serve with cheese.

BASIL PESTO

MAKES ABOUT 1 CUP

1 CUP PACKED FRESH BASIL LEAVES

1 CLOVE GARLIC, PEELED

2 OUNCES PARMIGIANO-REGGIANO, CUT INTO SMALL CHUNKS

¼ CUP PINE NUTS

½ CUP EXTRA VIRGIN OLIVE OIL

SALT AND FRESHLY GROUND BLACK PEPPER

Prepare a small bowl of ice water. Bring a 2-quart saucepan of water to a boil. Drop in the basil leaves and fish them out with tongs after 30 seconds. Transfer them to the ice water for a couple of minutes. Drain and press with paper towels to dry. Coarsely chop them.

Turn on a food processor. Drop in the garlic through the feed tube. When the garlic is minced, stop the machine, scrape down the sides, and place the basil, cheese, and pine nuts in the machine. Process until finely ground. With the machine running, slowly pour in the olive oil. Scrape down the sides of the work bowl, season with salt and pepper, transfer to a container, and refrigerate for at least 30 minutes.

Many cooks have a quick raw tomato sauce in their repertoire for summer. For this one, from a member of LVIS, the interesting touch is using a box grater to release the tomato pulp. It suggests the way they rub tomatoes on coarse toast in Spain to make the crostini they call pan con tomate. Here the bread crumbs also work their magic in sopping up and distributing the vibrant tomato juices.

SERVES 6

IMPROVEMENT: A bulb of burrata, finely chopped and including any liquid that oozes out, is a nice addition to this pasta dish.

Pasta with Uncooked Tomato Sauce

BARBARA LAMBERT

½ CUP PLAIN BREAD CRUMBS

5 TABLESPOONS EXTRA VIRGIN OLIVE OIL

ZEST OF ½ LEMON

4 LARGE RIPE TOMATOES

SALT

2 CLOVES GARLIC, FINELY CHOPPED

12 OUNCES SPAGHETTI OR PENNE

1 CUP FRESH BASIL LEAVES, CUT INTO CHIFFONADE

FRESHLY GROUND BLACK PEPPER

In a small bowl, mix the bread crumbs with 1 tablespoon of the oil. Place in a small skillet and cook over medium heat, stirring, until the crumbs are lightly browned, 2 to 3 minutes. Stir in the lemon zest. Set aside.

Core and halve 2 of the tomatoes and rub them against the large holes of a box grater held over a bowl to catch the pulp and juice. Discard the skin. Peel and core the remaining tomatoes and chop them into ½-inch dice. Add to the bowl. Work about ½ teaspoon salt into the garlic to form a paste, then add to the tomatoes. Let stand for 2 hours.

Bring a large pot of salted water to a boil. Cook the spaghetti until it is al dente, about 6 minutes; add another minute or two for penne. Drain and place in a large serving bowl. Fold all but a few tablespoons of the basil into the tomato mixture. Tip the bowl of tomatoes to one side so the juices gather and, using a large spoon, dip out several large spoonfuls of the juices from the bowl, add to the spaghetti, and toss to mix. Season the pasta with salt and pepper.

Add the rest of the tomato mixture to the pasta along with the remaining olive oil and toss to mix well. To serve from the bowl, scatter the bread crumbs on top, followed by the remaining basil, and serve. Or divide the pasta among individual soup plates and top each with the bread crumbs and basil.

Butterflied Leg of Lamb

BONNIE KRUPINSKI

1 CUP DRY RED WINE

1 CUP BEEF OR VEGETABLE STOCK

2 TABLESPOONS RED WINE VINEGAR

1 TABLESPOON FINELY MINCED ONION

1 TABLESPOON FRESH ROSEMARY LEAVES

1 TABLESPOON FRESH MARJORAM LEAVES

1 LARGE BAY LEAF, CRUMBLED

1 TEASPOON SALT

½ TEASPOON GROUND GINGER

1 LEG OF LAMB, SIX TO SEVEN POUNDS, BONED AND BUTTERFLIED

LEMON WEDGES FOR SERVING

Combine everything except the lamb and lemon wedges in a 2-quart saucepan. Bring to a simmer and cook for 20 minutes. Let cool for 30 minutes.

Two to three hours before you plan to serve the lamb, place it in a bowl or dish large enough to hold it, pour the wine mixture over it, and let it marinate in a cool place, turning once.

Heat a grill, preferably using hardwood charcoal. Remove the lamb from the marinade and reserve the marinade. Grill the lamb, turning several times and basting with the marinade as it cooks. You will need 30 to 40 minutes for medium-rare, but note that because the meat is thicker in some parts than others, you may want to carve off portions as they are done or, if some guests prefer the lamb more well-cooked, leave it to cook longer.

Transfer the lamb to a cutting board and let rest for 20 minutes before carving. Arrange on a platter and serve with lemon wedges.

IMPROVEMENT: For a smaller family dinner, you can buy a half leg, butterflied.

Bonnie and Ben Krupinski, prominent and generous members of the East Hampton community for decades, were loyal, giving supporters of LVIS, as well as of many other organizations. They perished, tragically, in a plane crash and are sorely missed. There had to be a recipe from Bonnie in this book, a project in which she was deeply involved at the time of her death. This is her recipe from the *LVIS Centennial Cookbook*.

SERVES 8

In midsummer the farm stands display sweet peppers in a kaleidoscope of colors from white and pale straw to deep purple, almost black. Gather a colorful array for this dish to serve alongside the lamb.

SERVES 6

Rainbow Peppers
FLORENCE FABRICANT

6 SWEET BELL PEPPERS, ASSORTED COLORS
4 TABLESPOONS EXTRA VIRGIN OLIVE OIL
SALT AND FRESHLY GROUND BLACK PEPPER

Halve, stem, and core the peppers. Cut each vertically in quarters. Brush them with 2 tablespoons of the olive oil.

Heat a grill. Place the pepper pieces crosswise on the grates or in a grilling basket. Grill, turning once, until lightly charred but still holding their shape, 3 to 4 minutes, depending on the heat of the grill. Remove the pieces when they're done and cut each in half again vertically. Place in a shallow bowl, toss with the remaining 2 tablespoons oil, and season with salt and pepper. Serve at once, or set aside and serve at room temperature.

IMPROVEMENT: Instead of grilling, you can slice the peppers vertically in ½-inch slivers and stir-fry them with some chopped fresh ginger.

Blackberries with Barbados Cream

JOAN EHREN

1 CUP HEAVY CREAM

1 CUP PLAIN GREEK YOGURT

⅓ CUP PACKED DARK BROWN SUGAR

3 CUPS FRESH BLACKBERRIES, OR A MIXTURE OF
BLACKBERRIES AND RASPBERRIES

FRESH MINT SPRIGS FOR GARNISH

A day in advance, whip the cream in a mixing bowl until softly peaked. Stir the yogurt to smooth it and fold into the whipped cream. Transfer to a shallow bowl. Sprinkle with the brown sugar, completely covering the top of the cream mixture. Cover and refrigerate for at least 12 hours.

Place the berries in a serving bowl and garnish with mint sprigs. Serve, with the sugared cream alongside. Or divide the berries among 4 to 6 stemmed goblets, spoon the sugared cream on top, garnish with mint sprigs, and serve.

IMPROVEMENT: The cream can crown other fruit, including sliced peaches or apricots. And a splash of rum on the berries is not a bad idea either.

This simple dessert from an LVIS member takes advantage of the stupendous, sweet blackberries that flourish in the area. "Barbados" refers to the brown sugar, a product of Caribbean plantations. In fact, a Colonial-era farm on Shelter Island, Sylvester Manor, was built mainly to supply food that could be shipped to the owners' plantation in Barbados, as part of the historically profitable, yet tragic, triangular trade.

SERVES 4 TO 6

BREAKFAST *for* WEEKEND GUESTS

East Hampton residents who might make do with toast and coffee for their own breakfast go to great lengths to satisfy houseguests in the morning. This sumptuous array for breakfast—or brunch—only requires that the oatmeal and pancakes be prepared à la minute; the rest can be made in advance. The menu can also be trimmed back with one or more dishes omitted. The usual brunch libations—mimosas, Bellinis, Bloody Marys, or Palomas (an increasingly popular option made with tequila, grapefruit, and soda)—can be poured.

Smoked Fish Rillettes • Savory Irish Oatmeal with Egg
Amber Waves Whole Wheat Pancakes
LVIS Sour Cream Coffee Cake • Beach Plum Jelly

Smoked Fish Rillettes

MICHAEL NOLAN, FRESNO RESTAURANT

Fresno Restaurant is a reliable destination year-round. The chef and owner makes this easy and alluring smoked fish spread year-round, too. Though he smokes his own local fluke to use for the rillettes, as the French call the spread, other, more easily obtained smoked fish can be substituted. The spread is excellent to whip up to serve with cocktails.

SERVES 6 TO 8

1 MEDIUM SHALLOT, MINCED

1½ POUNDS SMOKED BLUEFISH, SMOKED MACKEREL,
    OR SMOKED TROUT, SKINNED

2 TABLESPOONS LEMON JUICE

½ CUP CRÈME FRAÎCHE OR SOUR CREAM

SALT

SLICES OF TOASTED BAGUETTE OR DARK BREAD FOR SERVING

Place the shallot in a medium bowl or, if minced in a food processor, leave it in the machine. Break the fish into 1-inch chunks and add to the bowl or the machine. By hand, mix the shallot and fish with a fork, reducing the fish to small pieces, or pulse the fish in the food processor until finely chopped; transfer the mixture to a large bowl.

Stir in the lemon juice and crème fraîche and season with salt. Place into two 1-cup canning jars, preferably low and squat, or into a crock or pint-size bowl. Refrigerate until ready to serve, and arrange slices of bread alongside.

Savory Irish Oatmeal with Egg

JACK CEGLIC

1 CUP DICED FRESH PINEAPPLE

1 TABLESPOON MINCED FRESH GINGER

1 CUP STEEL-CUT IRISH OATS

SALT

1 TABLESPOON UNSALTED BUTTER

4 LARGE EGGS

Divide the pineapple and ginger among four individual serving bowls. Set aside.

Bring 4 cups water to a boil in a 3-quart saucepan. Reduce the heat to low and stir in the oats. Simmer until silky, stirring occasionally, about 20 minutes. Remove from the heat, season lightly with salt, cover, and set aside.

Melt the butter in a large skillet over medium heat and cook the eggs sunny-side up.

Stir the oatmeal and spoon it over the fruit in the bowls. Top each serving with a fried egg, dust lightly with salt, and serve.

IMPROVEMENT: Other fruit, like mango, ripe peaches, or berries can be used.

Jack Ceglic, an artist who specializes in portraits, is an accomplished cook. He was also one of the founders of the Dean & DeLuca fancy food stores, which once had an outlet in East Hampton, in a building that had been a post office and then a movie theater. This recipe elevates mere oatmeal to special occasion fare.

SERVES 4

Amanda Merrow and Katie Baldwin founded Amber Waves Farm in Amagansett in 2009 after completing an agricultural program at Quail Hill Farm nearby. Their goal was to reintroduce wheat as a local crop. In addition to wheat, the farm now cultivates a diversified array of organic vegetables on ten acres and is sustained through a CSA (community-supported agriculture, like a co-op). It also runs educational programs. The Mill House Inn in East Hampton buys the farm's wheat flour to make its delicious breakfast pancakes.

SERVES 4 TO 6

Amber Waves Whole Wheat Pancakes

MILL HOUSE INN

1½ CUPS WHOLE WHEAT FLOUR

1 TEASPOON BAKING POWDER

½ TEASPOON SALT

¼ TEASPOON GROUND CINNAMON

⅛ TEASPOON GROUND ALLSPICE

⅛ TEASPOON GROUND CLOVES

⅛ TEASPOON GROUND NUTMEG

1 LARGE EGG

⅔ CUP BUTTERMILK

1 TABLESPOON PURE MAPLE SYRUP, PLUS WARM MAPLE SYRUP
    FOR SERVING

½ TEASPOON VANILLA EXTRACT

1 TABLESPOON UNSALTED BUTTER

Preheat the oven to 200°F.

In a small bowl, whisk together the flour, baking powder, salt, cinnamon, allspice, cloves, and nutmeg. Set aside.

In a large bowl, beat the egg until well mixed. Beat in the buttermilk, the tablespoon of maple syrup, and the vanilla. Fold the reserved dry ingredients into the wet ingredients just enough to combine. The batter will be thick. Let the batter rest for 10 minutes.

Melt half the butter to coat the bottom of a heavy cast-iron skillet or griddle and heat over medium heat until the cooking surface is hot. Ladle scant ¼-cup portions of the batter onto the pan or griddle, leaving space for spreading. Cook the pancakes until browned on the bottom, about 3 minutes, then turn them and add more butter to the pan. Reduce the heat to low. Cook until the second side has browned, about 2 minutes. Transfer the pancakes to a platter and place in the oven to keep warm until ready to serve. Serve with warm maple syrup.

This recipe is from an LVIS member. She and her sister, Pam Cataletto, are longtime chairs of the LVIS Fair, and they can be counted on to bring baked goods to fair-planning meetings as an enticement for members to attend.

SERVES 12

LVIS Sour Cream Coffee Cake

BONNIE PIZZORNO

1 CUP FINELY CHOPPED WALNUTS

⅔ CUP PACKED LIGHT BROWN SUGAR

1 TEASPOON GROUND CINNAMON

2½ CUPS ALL-PURPOSE FLOUR

1 TABLESPOON BAKING POWDER

1 TEASPOON BAKING SODA

1 TEASPOON SALT

8 OUNCES (2 STICKS) UNSALTED BUTTER, SOFTENED, PLUS 1½ TEASPOONS FOR THE PAN

1 CUP GRANULATED SUGAR

3 LARGE EGGS

1 CUP SOUR CREAM

1 TEASPOON VANILLA EXTRACT

Preheat the oven to 325°F.

In a small bowl, combine the walnuts, brown sugar, and cinnamon. In another small bowl, whisk the flour, baking powder, baking soda, and salt.

Use the 1½ teaspoons of butter to grease a 10-inch Bundt pan. Sprinkle a little of the walnut mixture in the bottom of the pan.

By hand or machine, beat the 8 ounces (2 sticks) butter, gradually adding the granulated sugar and beating until very light. Beat in the eggs one at a time. Stir in one-third of the flour mixture, then half the sour cream, another third of the flour, the rest of the sour cream, and then the remaining flour mixture. Stir in the vanilla. Spoon one-third of the batter into the Bundt pan, sprinkle with half of the remaining walnut mixture, then another third of the batter, the rest of the walnuts, and the remaining batter.

Bake for about 1 hour, until a cake tester comes out clean. Let cool in the pan before unmolding.

IMPROVEMENT: If an uneaten portion of the cake becomes stale, slices can be toasted or pieces can be used to make a bread pudding, following the Doughnut Pudding recipe on page 142.

Beach Plum Jelly
ROSITA MEDLER

2 QUARTS RIPE BEACH PLUMS

6 CUPS SUGAR

3 OUNCES (ABOUT ⅓ CUP) LIQUID PECTIN OR
   1 PACKET (1.75 OUNCES) PECTIN POWDER

Rinse the plums in a colander, picking out and discarding any leaves or bits of stem. Place them in a large pot, at least 4 quarts. Crush the plums using a potato masher. Add 2½ cups water, bring to a boil, reduce the heat and simmer, covered, for 30 minutes, stirring occasionally.

Sterilize six 8-ounce or eight 6-ounce glass jelly jars and new lids in boiling water and set aside.

Place the colander over a 3-quart saucepan. Have a dampened cloth jelly bag ready or line the colander with several layers of cheesecloth. Pour the contents of the pot with the plums into the cloth. Remove the colander and squeeze the juice into the saucepan. There should be about 3½ cups of juice. A little more or less is fine. Discard the rest of the plum mixture. Add the sugar and mix well. Place over high heat and bring to a boil, stirring constantly. Immediately stir in the pectin and boil hard 1 minute, still stirring constantly.

Remove from the heat, skim off the foam with a metal spoon, and pour into the jars. For shelf-stable storage you can seal the jars with a thin layer of hot, melted paraffin. They will keep for a year. Alternatively, prepare a pot of boiling water large enough to accommodate the jars. Cap the jars with their lids, not screwing them on very tightly, and process them in the boiling water bath for 10 minutes, let cool, then tighten the lids. Without any paraffin or processing in a water bath, the filled jars will keep for 3 months in the refrigerator.

Beach plums grow on bushes, usually shoulder height, in sandy soil near the beaches in Amagansett and Napeague. Some years they're abundant, others not. They cannot be eaten raw as they are extremely tannic. This recipe for jelly is from an LVIS member who has made it for decades. At the LVIS Fair, jars of her jelly invariably sell out.

MAKES 6 CUPS

SUMMER DINNER PARTY

It's so easy to be tempted by fresh produce and seafood, especially in summer, and to be inspired to share them with close friends. Big entertaining is common in the Hamptons. But an intimate dinner for four or six, like this one, allows the host or hostess to interact with guests and have a real conversation instead of the fleeting "hi and how are you" of cocktail party chatter. This menu deserves a well-bred white wine, a full-bodied chardonnay with a touch of crispness from having been cultivated near the sea, perhaps, or even a Riesling with some richness.

Southside Cocktail • Heirloom Tomato Bisque
Broiled Fish with Anchovy Butter
Herbed New Potatoes with Fresh Peas • Peach Tartlets

MEMBERS ONLY   EST. 1916
DEVON YACHT CLUB PIER
NO ONE UNDER THE AGE OF 12 PERMITTED WITHOUT AN ADULT

Southside Cocktail
DEVON YACHT CLUB

2 OUNCES SIMPLE SYRUP (RECIPE FOLLOWS)

4 OUNCES WHITE RUM

2 OUNCES LEMON JUICE

1 OUNCE LIME JUICE

COUPLE SPRIGS OF MINT

Prepare the simple syrup.

In a cocktail shaker, shake together the rum, simple syrup, and citrus juices with ice. Strain into 2 stemmed cocktail glasses. Garnish with the mint.

IMPROVEMENT: To serve the drink Devon style do not strain the mixture. Whirl it in a blender with a cup of ice cubes.

SIMPLE SYRUP

MAKES ABOUT ½ CUP

½ CUP SUGAR

½ CUP WATER

Mix the sugar and water together in a small saucepan. Bring to a simmer and cook for 2 to 3 minutes, just until the sugar has dissolved and the syrup is clear. Transfer to a jar or container, cover, and refrigerate. It will keep about a month.

The Southside's only competition as the perfect summer quaff is a gin and tonic. This recipe comes from the Devon Yacht Club on Gardiner's Bay, which is known for its Fourth of July fireworks display. The Southside is the club's signature drink, but made with white rum instead of the usual gin, and with prepared sour mix. Keep the rum but use a combination of simple syrup and citrus juice to replace the mix.

SERVES 2

Heirloom Tomato Bisque
COVE HOLLOW TAVERN

1 TABLESPOON UNSALTED BUTTER

2 TABLESPOONS EXTRA VIRGIN OLIVE OIL

½ CUP CHOPPED ONION

¼ CUP CHOPPED CARROT

⅔ CUP CHOPPED FENNEL BULB

2 CLOVES GARLIC, SLICED

1 BAY LEAF

SALT AND FRESHLY GROUND BLACK PEPPER

2 TABLESPOONS ALL-PURPOSE FLOUR

½ CUP DRY SHERRY

3 POUNDS RED AND/OR YELLOW HEIRLOOM TOMATOES,
    CORED AND CHOPPED

3 SPRIGS THYME

⅓ CUP HEAVY CREAM

This restaurant, in a roadside cottage in East Hampton, is a branch of a popular Shelter Island spot, Vine Street Café. The menus are similar. Heed the instruction to use heirloom tomatoes, which are cultivated on local farms and widely sold on their stands, for their incomparable flavor.

SERVES 4 TO 6

Melt the butter with the oil in a heavy 3- to 4-quart saucepan over medium-low heat. Add the onion, carrot, fennel, garlic, and bay leaf. Season with salt and pepper and cook until the onion is translucent, about 3 minutes. Stir in the flour and cook for about 2 minutes. Stir in the sherry and cook just until the mixture has thickened, about 2 minutes.

Add the tomatoes and thyme and continue cooking, stirring from time to time, until the tomatoes collapse and the carrots are tender, 20 to 30 minutes. Stir in the cream and simmer for 5 minutes. Remove from the heat and let cool for 20 minutes. Puree in a blender (you may have to do this in two shifts).

Return the soup to the saucepan and bring to a simmer. Serve immediately, or set aside and reheat before serving. Adjust the salt and pepper as needed. You can thin the soup with a little water if you find it to be too thick.

IMPROVEMENT: The soup can be made without the cream. It can also be served chilled.

Elizabeth "Boots" Lamb was a member of LVIS and an active real estate broker in town. She and her husband, Joseph Condie Lamb, an artist, lived in a nineteenth-century house opposite Town Pond that was once owned by the artist Thomas Moran. The Lambs called it The Studio. Today it is known as the Moran House and, with the help of a foundation, it has been restored and is open to visitors. An education center at Guild Hall, the cultural center nearby, is named for Mrs. Lamb. Her fish recipe, which was in the *LVIS Centennial Cookbook,* called for weakfish, sometimes referred to as sea trout. Weakfish harvests seem to come and go in cycles. Bluefish, which demands utter freshness—about the only way you'll find it on Eastern Long Island—makes a fine substitute here. It's an assertive creature, a fierce predator in the water and richly flavored on the plate. Anchovy butter tames it perfectly.

SERVES 6

Broiled Fish with Anchovy Butter
MRS. CONDIE LAMB

7 TABLESPOONS UNSALTED BUTTER, SOFTENED

6 ANCHOVY FILLETS, WELL DRAINED

1 TEASPOON LEMON JUICE

1 CUCUMBER, PEELED

6 BLUEFISH FILLETS, EACH 6 OUNCES, WITH SKIN (OR 3 FILLETS, HALVED)

1 CUP DRY WHITE WINE

SALT AND FRESHLY GROUND BLACK PEPPER

1 TABLESPOON MINCED FLAT-LEAF PARSLEY

LEMON WEDGES FOR SERVING

In a medium bowl, mash the butter and anchovy fillets together until the mixture becomes a smooth paste. Work in the lemon juice. Divide into 7 portions and set aside. Cut the cucumber in half lengthwise and use a spoon—a grapefruit spoon if you have one—to scrape out the seeds. Slice the cucumber fairly thin.

Line a rimmed baking sheet (large enough to hold all the fish) with foil. Place the fish on the pan, skin-side down, and drizzle the fillets with ½ cup of the wine. Set aside for 1 hour.

Preheat the broiler. Spread each fillet with one of the portions of anchovy butter. Place the fish under the broiler and cook just until it turns opaque, 7 to 10 minutes.

Meanwhile, prepare a warm platter. Remove the fish to the platter and tent with foil. Scatter the cucumber slices in the hot pan and add the remaining anchovy butter and ½ cup wine. Run under the broiler for about 2 minutes, until the cucumbers just turn limp. Stir the mixture in the pan and spoon over the fish. Season with salt and pepper if needed. Scatter with the parsley and serve with lemon wedges.

IMPROVEMENT: Fluke, flounder, black sea bass, or mackerel fillets can be used.

Herbed New Potatoes with Fresh Peas

CRAIG CLAIBORNE

1 CUP SHELLED FRESH ENGLISH PEAS (1 POUND IN THE POD)

1½ POUNDS SMALL NEW POTATOES, RED OR WHITE

SALT

2 TABLESPOONS UNSALTED BUTTER

¼ CUP CRÈMF FRAÎCHE

FRESHLY GROUND BLACK PEPPER

1 TABLESPOON FRESH BASIL CUT INTO CHIFFONADE

1 TABLESPOON MINCED FLAT-LEAF PARSLEY LEAVES

Place the peas and potatoes in a medium saucepan, cover with salted water, and bring to a boil over high heat. Reduce the heat and simmer until both are tender, about 20 minutes. Meanwhile, prepare a 1 quart bowl of ice water with a strainer suspended in it. Drain the peas and potatoes and remove the potatoes to a bowl. Place the peas in the strainer, submerged in the ice water, to chill them. Drain. Return the potatoes to the saucepan and cover. Set the peas aside at room temperature.

Add the butter and crème fraîche to the potatoes and heat gently for about 5 minutes to warm them. Add the peas and continue to cook for another 5 minutes. Remove from the heat, stir, season with salt and pepper, shower with parsley and basil, and serve.

IMPROVEMENT: In place of the butter and crème fraîche, you can use 4 tablespoons extra virgin olive oil.

As the food editor of *The New York Times*, Craig Claiborne was not only responsible for creating the restaurant reviewing system still used at the newspaper, but also for discovering countless young chefs and putting their careers in the spotlight. He was one of many *Times* writers and editors with homes in East Hampton. His parties were legendary, gatherings that often included visiting culinary dignitaries from far and wide. And he was a great cook.

SERVES 4 TO 6

Buy local and you will be guaranteed tree-ripened peaches in midsummer. In this simple dessert recipe from Cameron Prather, one of the food stylists for this book, the peaches are not even cooked but simply layered over a veneer of mascarpone onto buttery pistachio shortbread tartlet shells. As for the honey, there are plenty of locally gathered varieties sold in the region.

SERVES 4

Peach Tartlets
CAMERON PRATHER

1½ TEASPOONS UNSALTED BUTTER, MELTED

½ CUP PLUS 1 TABLESPOON SALTED SHELLED PISTACHIOS
   (OR UNSALTED PISTACHIOS PLUS ¼ TEASPOON SALT)

⅔ CUP ALL-PURPOSE FLOUR

6 TABLESPOONS PACKED LIGHT BROWN SUGAR

½ TEASPOON VANILLA EXTRACT

4 TABLESPOONS COLD UNSALTED BUTTER, DICED

1 CUP MASCARPONE CHEESE

¼ TEASPOON SALT

3 TABLESPOONS HONEY

4 RIPE MEDIUM PEACHES, PITTED AND SLICED ½ INCH THICK

Preheat the oven to 350°F. Use the melted butter to grease 4 loose-bottomed 4-inch round tartlet pans.

Place the pistachios in a food processor and pulse until finely ground but not turned to paste. Remove 1 tablespoon and set aside. Add the flour, brown sugar, and vanilla to the food processor and pulse to form a crumbly mixture. Add the cold butter and pulse just until the mixture starts to clump. Scoop out the mixture onto a work surface and form it into a disk. Divide it into four pieces and press the mixture into the bottom and sides of each of the tartlet pans. Place in the oven and bake until lightly browned, about 12 minutes. Remove from the oven and let cool.

Mix the mascarpone cheese with the salt and 2 tablespoons of the honey in a small bowl. Spread it in each of the cooled shells. Toss the peach slices with the remaining 1 tablespoon honey and arrange them, overlapping, on the mascarpone. Scatter with the reserved pistachios.

IMPROVEMENT: Consider this recipe to be a springboard inviting other fruit, including fresh plums, apricots, and figs, and other nuts, like pecans and walnuts, to be used.

Clockwise from above: Clinton Academy, the birthplace of the LVIS, as it looks today. In the village's business district, White's Apothecary is one of many buildings that retain the charm of more provincial days gone by. The broad pavilion at Main Beach, which has been a bathing destination since the 1870s. Montauk Lighthouse, an iconic landmark commissioned by George Washington. Many visitors' first glimpse of East Hampton is the still-rather-quaint Long Island Rail Road station. The Osborn-Jackson House is home to the East Hampton Historical Society, which has long been an informal partner of sorts with the LVIS in preserving all that's most beautiful about the village and its heritage. LongHouse Reserve, a 16-acre garden and open-air sculpture site founded by Jack Lenor Larsen.

The kitchen and bar in the historic Maidstone Hotel in East Hampton has been led by its share of fine chefs over the years. Michael Field and Tom Cowman were two of the notables back in the days when it was called the Maidstone Arms. Now it is owned by Jenny Baker, a Swedish hotelier, and Jonathan Baker, an entrepreneur. The building, a Greek Revival mansion, was built overlooking Town Pond by the Osborne family before the Civil War. It was converted into a country inn about a hundred years ago. The Bakers completely renovated it and modernized the rooms after they took over. In summer, they serve this watermelon-infused version of a refreshing Moscow mule. For a picnic, bring the chilled ginger beer unopened and add it on the spot. Cans are lighter to carry than bottles and will help keep everything colder. And you do not need the traditional copper mugs for serving.

SERVES 6

Watermelon Moscow Mule
THE MAIDSTONE HOTEL

3 CUPS (1-INCH CUBES) WATERMELON

1½ CUPS VODKA, CHILLED

JUICE OF 3 LIMES, CHILLED

3 OUNCES AGAVE SYRUP, OR TO TASTE (SIMPLE SYRUP, PAGE 74, CAN BE USED)

3 (12-OUNCE) CANS OR BOTTLES GINGER BEER, CHILLED

Muddle half the watermelon in a mixing glass or pitcher. Spear the remaining watermelon cubes on six 4-inch bamboo skewers and set aside.

Add the vodka, lime juice, and as much agave syrup as pleases you to the container with the muddled watermelon and mix. Add ice and stir to mix well. Strain into 6 copper mugs or rocks glasses filled with ice. Top each off with half a can or bottle of ginger beer. Garnish with the skewered watermelon.

IMPROVEMENT: It won't be a Moscow mule, but if you use gin instead of vodka, omit the syrup, and add good tonic water in place of ginger beer, you'll have refreshing watermelon gin and tonics.

The LVIS FAIR

The LVIS Fair is one of the most highly anticipated summer events in East Hampton. The first Fair was held in 1896 and featured the society's first cookbook. The vintage photo here shows the Fair in the summer of 1915. This cookbook, in celebration of the LVIS's 125th Anniversary, is the organization's thirteenth. The Fair continues to be a major source of funding to support the commitments that the LVIS makes to the community.

HIGH-SEASON BUFFET

With a guest list that exceeds eight to ten, entertaining buffet-style instead of serving a sit-down dinner makes sense. You need to provide only one plate, one glass, and a knife and fork per person, and having someone to help with service is less necessary. Guests can pour their own drinks, too. In season, if the weather cooperates, you can take advantage of an outdoor setting. But there is a trick to making all this happen smoothly. First is to select food that does not need to be served piping hot. And second, see to it that there are enough places for guests to sit, preferably with some kind of table at hand on which to perch a plate and a glass. And be sure to provide generous-size cloth napkins for laps. For a party like this, have red, white, and rosé wines, along with water, juices, and, if you think they're needed, spirits, on hand. Bottles with screw tops are convenient.

Rosé Cocktail • Tomato Sandwiches • "Oven-Fried" Garlic Chicken
Grilled Montauk Tuna Stuffed with Herbs and Tapenade
Petits Farcis (Stuffed Tomatoes) • Classic Potato Salad
Nana's Rum-Laced Brownies

The rosé wines made by Wölffer Estate in Sagaponack are popular summertime quaffs in the region and beyond. This fruit- and herb-driven cocktail was created by the winery. But other rosés, from Channing Daughters nearby, for example, or from producers farther afield, can be poured as well.

SERVES 4

Rosé Cocktail
WÖLFFER KITCHEN

½ PINT RASPBERRIES

8 FRESH MINT LEAVES

4 SLICES CUCUMBER

2 OUNCES SIMPLE SYRUP (PAGE 74) OR AGAVE SYRUP

2 OUNCES CHAMBORD LIQUEUR, OTHER BLACK RASPBERRY LIQUEUR, OR CRÈME DE CASSIS

JUICE OF 2 LEMONS

6 OUNCES COGNAC

2 CUPS ROSÉ WINE, CHILLED

2 SLICES ORANGE, HALVED

In a large cocktail shaker or a quart-size covered jar, muddle half the raspberries, the mint, and cucumber with the simple syrup. Add the Chambord, lemon juice, and Cognac. Add ice until it half fills the container and add the rosé wine. Shake.

Strain into 4 large wine glasses, add the remaining raspberries and the orange slices, and serve.

IMPROVEMENT: Consider using gin in place of the Cognac. Wölffer makes one.

"Oven-Fried" Garlic Chicken

GEORGE HIRSCH

1 TEASPOON DRIED SAGE

1 TEASPOON DRIED OREGANO

1 TEASPOON DRIED THYME

1 TEASPOON SWEET PAPRIKA

1½ TEASPOONS GARLIC POWDER

SEA SALT AND FRESHLY GROUND BLACK PEPPER

12 CHICKEN THIGHS WITH SKIN AND BONES

JUICE OF ½ LEMON

1 TABLESPOON GRAPESEED OIL

1¼ CUPS ALL-PURPOSE FLOUR

Combine the sage, oregano, thyme, paprika, garlic powder, and salt and pepper to taste in a shallow bowl. Coat the chicken with the seasoning mixture, sprinkle with the lemon juice, and place on a platter. Cover and refrigerate for at least 30 minutes or overnight.

Preheat the oven to 425°F.

Select a roasting pan with sides that will hold the chicken in a single layer without crowding. Brush the bottom of the pan with the oil. Place the flour in a bag or a bowl and coat the chicken with the flour one piece at a time, shaking off any excess. Arrange the chicken in a single layer in the pan, skin-side up. Bake for 15 minutes. Reduce the oven temperature to 350°F and continue baking until the chicken is crisp and golden brown. Let the chicken rest for at least 5 minutes or let it come to room temperature before serving.

IMPROVEMENT: The recipe can be doubled or tripled.

"Who doesn't like fried chicken?" That's the question posed by this chef and cooking instructor based in Southampton. But like most of us, he admits to not wanting to take the time and effort to prepare it, to say nothing about the health concerns. His solution is to bake it. The result is excellent served at room temperature. Though his original recipe called for a whole chicken, cut up, he also advised that using all dark meat produces the best results, so that's what you have here.

SERVES 6 OR MORE

This chef has enjoyed a career of haute cuisine, but lately he has turned his attention to more crowd-pleasing fare. He started with a burger place in Sag Harbor, and the success of that led to an excellent pizzeria down the street, building on the delicious pizzas he has been making at his casual New York restaurant L'Amico. As a resident, he's a fan of the fish that come to the Montauk docks, especially the fresh tuna. For this recipe he usually takes a tuna steak and cuts a pocket in it to fill with the stuffing. Making individual roulades makes it easier to serve on a buffet table but does not compromise the recipe. You can serve whole roulades, one per person, or halve them to serve more guests.

SERVES 6 TO 12

Grilled Montauk Tuna Stuffed with Herbs and Tapenade

LAURENT TOURONDEL, LT BURGER, SAG PIZZA

¼ CUP BLACK OLIVE TAPENADE

1 CUP FRESH BASIL LEAVES, COARSELY CHOPPED

1 ANCHOVY, RINSED AND CHOPPED

½ TEASPOON MINCED HOT RED CHILE, OR TO TASTE

2 TABLESPOONS CAPERS IN VINEGAR, RINSED AND CHOPPED

3 (12- TO 14-OUNCE, 1-INCH-THICK) BLUEFIN, YELLOWFIN, OR BIGEYE TUNA STEAKS, PREFERABLY LOCAL

⅓ CUP EXTRA VIRGIN OLIVE OIL, PLUS A FEW TABLESPOONS FOR SERVING

1 TABLESPOON FINELY CHOPPED GARLIC

1½ TABLESPOONS CHOPPED FRESH ROSEMARY LEAVES

2 TABLESPOONS CHOPPED FRESH OREGANO LEAVES

1 TABLESPOON CRACKED BLACK PEPPERCORNS

SALT AND FRESHLY GROUND BLACK PEPPER

1 LEMON, CUT INTO 6 WEDGES, OR 2 LEMONS, CUT INTO 12 WEDGES

Combine the tapenade, basil, anchovy, chile, and capers in a small bowl.

Use a sharp slicing knife to slice each tuna steak all the way through horizontally, making 6 steaks each about ½ inch thick. Place a couple of tablespoons of the tapenade mixture in the center of each slice of tuna, roll up the fish, and tie it with butcher's twine in three places.

Mix the olive oil with the garlic, rosemary, oregano, and peppercorns in a medium bowl. Place the stuffed tuna steaks in the bowl and turn them to coat with the olive oil mixture. Cover and refrigerate for 4 hours.

Light a grill. Remove the roulades from the marinade and season with salt and pepper. Grill the roulades, turning them a few times and letting them cook for 2 to 3 minutes after each turn, for 8 to 10

minutes total. The tuna should retain some pinkness. The roulades can also be cooked in a grill pan on top of the stove, or broiled, for the same amount of time. Let cool briefly, then carefully snip off the trussing. If desired, before removing the twine, each roulade can be cut in half or into thick slices. Transfer to a platter or to individual plates, drizzle with a little extra olive oil and salt and pepper, and serve with lemon wedges.

IMPROVEMENT: Swordfish can be used in place of the tuna.

In Nice, on the French Riviera, the outdoor market sells small tomatoes, zucchini, eggplant, and peppers that are usually stuffed with bread crumbs, lamb, and herbs. Georgette Farkas, who spends considerable time in East Hampton, and who owns Rotisserie Georgette in Manhattan, takes advantage of the local vegetable crop with her meatless version of the Niçoise specialty. Though she uses only tomatoes in this recipe, if you can find small round zucchini, small bell peppers, or baby eggplants, you can share the filling with those, too.

SERVES 12

IMPROVEMENT: You can make these bite-size by using a few dozen cherry tomatoes. Slice about ¼ inch off the bottoms of the tomatoes. (Using the little tomatoes upside-down guarantees that they will be stable on a serving platter.) Scoop out the insides with a small spoon. Finely chop what you remove from the tomatoes and add it to the quinoa mixture. Fill the tomatoes and serve without baking.

Petits Farcis (Stuffed Tomatoes)

GEORGETTE FARKAS, ROTISSERIE GEORGETTE

12 SMALL RIPE TOMATOES, EACH ABOUT 2½ INCHES IN DIAMETER
SALT AND FRESHLY GROUND BLACK PEPPER
3 TABLESPOONS EXTRA VIRGIN OLIVE OIL
¼ CUP FINELY CHOPPED ONION
6 CUPS VEGETABLE BROTH
1 CUP QUINOA
½ CUP PESTO (PAGE 54)

Slice ½ inch off the tops of the tomatoes; reserve the tops. Scoop out the flesh, seeds, and liquid from the tomatoes and reserve them for another use. Season the insides of the tomatoes with salt and pepper. Place the tomatoes upside down on a platter to drain.

Heat 2 tablespoons of the oil in a 3-quart saucepan over medium heat. Add the onion and sauté, stirring, until translucent, about 2 minutes. Add the vegetable broth, season with salt, and bring to a boil. Stir in the quinoa, reduce the heat to very low, cover the pan, and simmer about 12 minutes, until the quinoa is just cooked through. Set aside, covered, for 10 minutes. Fluff with a fork and fold in the pesto. Fill the tomatoes with the quinoa; do not pack the stuffing in, as it will expand a bit during baking. Replace the tops of the tomatoes.

Preheat the oven to 350°F. Brush a baking dish that can hold the tomatoes in a single layer with the remaining 1 tablespoon olive oil. Place the tomatoes in the dish. Bake for 15 minutes. Remove the tops of the tomatoes and set them aside so they do not overcook. Continue baking the stuffed tomatoes for another 15 minutes, until the quinoa is lightly browned.

Replace the tops on the tomatoes and arrange on a serving dish.

Classic Potato Salad

BONNY REIFF-SMITH

2 POUNDS MEDIUM YUKON GOLD POTATOES, WASHED
   (ABOUT 10 POTATOES)

½ CUP FINELY CHOPPED VIDALIA ONION

¼ CUP FINELY CHOPPED SHALLOTS

3 TABLESPOONS RICE VINEGAR OR CIDER VINEGAR

SALT AND FRESHLY GROUND BLACK PEPPER

1½ CUPS MAYONNAISE, STORE-BOUGHT OR HOMEMADE,
   AT ROOM TEMPERATURE

4 LARGE HARD-COOKED EGG YOLKS (OPTIONAL)

3 TABLESPOONS MINCED FRESH CHIVES

Place the potatoes in a large saucepan, cover with water, and bring to a boil. Reduce the heat to low and simmer until the potatoes are tender when pierced with a paring knife, about 20 minutes. Drain and, as soon as the potatoes are cool enough to handle, cut them into 1-inch pieces, with the skin.

Place the onion and shallots in a large bowl. Put the warm potatoes on top and douse with the vinegar. Season with salt and abundant pepper and fold all the ingredients together.

Place the mayonnaise in a separate bowl and stir. Crush the egg yolks, if using, and add them to the mayonnaise. Fold the mayonnaise mixture into the potatoes. Transfer to a serving dish, shower with chives, and serve.

IMPROVEMENT: In place of mayonnaise, consider using aioli (page 89).

This LVIS member, an excellent cook and a cookbook committee stalwart, knows when it's best to keep things simple. When we needed a potato salad for this book, she volunteered hers, a keeper.

SERVES 6 TO 8

Nana's Rum-Laced Brownies

RALPH AND RICKY LAUREN

"Ralph loved Nana's brownies so much that he offered to put a brownie department in his stores so he would not have to wait until his October birthday when she would make another batch for him," said Ricky Lauren, Ralph's wife. When Nana, her mother, stayed with them at their oceanfront estate in Montauk, she made the brownies for the family all summer long. These days the brownies are served at the Polo Bar, the Ralph Lauren restaurants, and in cafés.

MAKES 4 DOZEN

8 OUNCES (2 STICKS) SALTED BUTTER, PLUS MORE FOR THE PAN
2 CUPS ALL-PURPOSE FLOUR, PLUS MORE FOR THE PAN
1½ TEASPOONS BAKING POWDER
PINCH OF SALT
6 OUNCES UNSWEETENED CHOCOLATE, CHOPPED INTO SMALL PIECES
3 CUPS SUGAR
6 LARGE EGGS
1 TABLESPOON VANILLA EXTRACT
1½ CUPS CHOPPED WALNUTS
RUM GLAZE (RECIPE FOLLOWS)
WALNUT HALVES FOR DECORATION

Preheat the oven to 375°F. Grease a 9 by 13-inch baking pan with butter. Dust with flour.

Place the flour in a small bowl and whisk in the baking powder and salt.

Place the butter, chocolate, and sugar in a medium saucepan over medium-low heat. When the butter and chocolate have melted, remove the pan from the heat and stir. In a large bowl, beat the eggs and vanilla until the eggs are smooth but have not become frothy. Stir in the chocolate mixture and the flour mixture. Fold in the chopped walnuts. Spread in the prepared pan.

Bake for 35 to 40 minutes, until a cake tester comes out almost clean. Remove from the oven and let cool, then spread on the rum glaze. Cut the brownies into 2-inch squares and place a walnut half on each. Refrigerate for 1 hour before serving.

RUM GLAZE

MAKES ENOUGH FOR ONE BATCH OF NANA'S RUM-LACED BROWNIES; ABOUT ¾ CUP

6 TABLESPOONS SALTED BUTTER

4 OUNCES UNSWEETENED CHOCOLATE, CHOPPED INTO SMALL PIECES

¼ CUP CONFECTIONERS' SUGAR

2 TEASPOONS VANILLA EXTRACT

3 TABLESPOONS DARK RUM OR BRANDY

In a medium saucepan, melt the butter and chocolate over low heat. Sift in the confectioners' sugar and blend it in. Stir in the vanilla and rum or brandy. The glaze should be used while still warm.

LABOR DAY GRILLING

Somehow, social gatherings around Labor Day weekend inevitably involve grilling. It's as evident in East Hampton as it is nationwide. The usual suspects, hot dogs and hamburgers, or a mess of ribs, are definitely crowd-pleasers and simple enough to execute, with condiments, sides, and all. Skewered meats are another option, as this menu demonstrates. Though some cookbooks will have you believe that you can grill everything on your menu, that's not the approach taken here. The main course lamb kebabs with their accompanying vegetable skewers will keep the grill busy. The rest of the menu is kitchen work, mostly done in advance. Keep guests' glasses filled with beer, red wine, and perhaps gin or vodka and tonics made with Sagaponack Farm Distillery spirits.

Pissaladière • Lamb and Summer Vegetable Kebabs
Grilled Corn with Mole Verde • Southern Plum Cobbler

Lamb and Summer Vegetable Kebabs

AMAGANSETT SEA SALT COMPANY

2 CUPS PLAIN YOGURT

8 TABLESPOONS EXTRA VIRGIN OLIVE OIL

6 TABLESPOONS LEMON JUICE

2 TEASPOONS LEMON ZEST

½ CUP CHOPPED FRESH ROSEMARY LEAVES

¼ CUP CHOPPED FRESH MINT LEAVES

2 TEASPOONS FINE SEA SALT

½ TEASPOON FRESHLY GROUND BLACK PEPPER

3 POUNDS TOP ROUND OF LAMB, CUT INTO 1½-INCH CUBES

3 MEDIUM GREEN OR YELLOW ZUCCHINI, CUT INTO WHEELS 1½ INCHES THICK

3 MEDIUM RED ONIONS, CUT INTO WEDGES 2 INCHES WIDE

1½ PINTS CHERRY TOMATOES, STEMS REMOVED

COARSE SEA SALT

Combine the yogurt, 6 tablespoons of the olive oil, the lemon juice and zest, rosemary, mint, fine sea salt, and pepper in a large bowl. Add the cubes of lamb, mix well, cover, and refrigerate at least 4 hours or overnight.

Place the zucchini, onions, and tomatoes in a large bowl, add the remaining 2 tablespoons olive oil, and toss to coat the vegetables. Set aside.

Preheat a grill or broiler. Thread the meat on metal or presoaked bamboo skewers. Thread the vegetables, alternating the varieties, on separate skewers. Grill or broil the lamb for 5 to 8 minutes, depending on the heat of your grill, turning once or twice, for medium-rare. Grill the vegetables for 6 to 8 minutes, until lightly charred.

Arrange the skewers on a large serving platter and dust with coarse sea salt.

IMPROVEMENT: By using two thin skewers side by side instead of just one for each kebab, you can guarantee that the ingredients will stay in place and not spin around as you turn the skewers.

The notion of hauling buckets of seawater to the shore, then letting it evaporate to produce natural sea salt, sounds practical yet borderline insane. But that's precisely what Steven and Natalie Judelson, residents of Amagansett, have been doing for years. And they've convinced the doubters. Their natural sea salt constantly wins accolades from important chefs and is sold nationwide. Their recipe for lamb kebabs calls for fine salt in the marinade and coarse salt for final seasoning.

SERVES 8

A Nashville native, the vivacious food expert Carla Hall is a fan of the Hamptons and a frequent visitor. Her plum cobbler may have a Southern accent, but it's appropriate in this area. Though most of the plums in the markets are California-grown, there are some small, local ones to be had in late summer. And coincidentally, Hall's pastry recipe is the same as the one used at the fine foods store Loaves & Fishes.

SERVES 8

IMPROVEMENT: Other fruit, including peaches—another classic—but also nectarines and apricots, suit this cobbler. It can also be served warm.

Southern Plum Cobbler
CARLA HALL

3½ POUNDS RIPE PLUMS, PITTED AND CUT INTO ½-INCH CHUNKS

3 TABLESPOONS FRESH ORANGE JUICE

½ CUP PACKED LIGHT BROWN SUGAR

¼ CUP GRANULATED SUGAR

2 TABLESPOONS CORNSTARCH

1 TABLESPOON LEMON JUICE

2 TEASPOONS ORANGE ZEST

¾ TEASPOON GROUND CINNAMON

¼ TEASPOON SALT

TWO-CRUST PASTRY (PAGE 39)

ALL-PURPOSE FLOUR FOR THE WORK SURFACE

1 LARGE EGG, BEATEN

Place an oven rack on the lowest position and preheat the oven to 450°F.

To make the filling, toss the plums, orange juice, both sugars, the cornstarch, lemon juice, orange zest, ½ teaspoon of the cinnamon, and the salt in a large bowl until well mixed. Let sit for at least 30 minutes while you prepare the crust.

On a lightly floured surface, roll out two-thirds of the pastry into a 12-inch circle. Fit into a 9-inch cast-iron skillet or a deep-dish pie plate and crimp the edges. Freeze until ready to fill. With the smaller disc of pie dough, break off almond-size pieces to form pebbly crumbles. Toss with the remaining ¼ teaspoon cinnamon until evenly coated. Refrigerate.

Whisk the egg with 2 tablespoons water in a small bowl and set aside. Spoon the plum mixture into the pastry-lined pan. Scatter the pie dough crumbles all over the top. Dab with the egg wash. Place the cobbler on a baking sheet and place on the lowest oven rack. Bake until the crust and topping are golden brown and the filling is bubbling, about 45 minutes. Cool completely in the pan on a wire rack.

VEGAN DINNER

Considering the wealth of vegetables in the area, putting together a vegetarian menu can be effortless. For some vegetarians, dairy, eggs, and even fish are acceptable, simplifying the planning. But a vegan meal is more restricted, avoiding all animal-sourced ingredients. Here's one game plan for a colorful array of dishes, none of which require vegan substitutes like nut-based "cheese." Some celebrities have contributed to this menu. When it comes to wine, it's best to select a white like a local chardonnay. Some red wines are "fined," or clarified, by using egg whites, something that vegans avoid, and it's difficult to know which.

Vegan Curried Cauliflower Soup
Poor Man's Caviar • Christie's Couscous
Moroccan Carrot Salad • Vanilla Date Smoothie
Cornmeal-Oatmeal Dark Chocolate Chip Cookies

The LVIS member who contributed this recipe did not highlight it as being vegan. Her original recipe called for chicken broth, not vegetable broth, but she pointed out that the substitution can be made to please a vegetarian. She may not have realized it was actually vegan.

SERVES 6

Vegan Curried Cauliflower Soup

JOAN McGIVERN

6 CLOVES GARLIC, MINCED

2 CUPS FINELY MINCED ONIONS

3 TABLESPOONS EXTRA VIRGIN OLIVE OIL

3 TABLESPOONS CURRY POWDER, OR TO TASTE

1 TABLESPOON GROUND CUMIN

6 CUPS VEGETABLE BROTH

4 CUPS CAULIFLOWER FLORETS (ABOUT 1 SMALL HEAD)

5 TABLESPOONS UNSWEETENED CANNED COCONUT MILK (NOT LIGHT)

¾ CUP UNSALTED PISTACHIOS, COARSELY CHOPPED

SALT AND FRESHLY GROUND BLACK PEPPER

Place the garlic and onions in a 4-quart saucepan. Add the oil and sauté over low heat until the garlic and onion are softened but not browned, about 3 minutes. Stir in the curry powder and cumin and sauté for another 5 minutes or so, until the spices are fragrant. Add 3 cups of the broth, increase the heat to medium, and simmer for 15 minutes. Add the cauliflower and the remaining 3 cups broth and continue to simmer until the cauliflower is very tender, 15 to 20 minutes more. Let cool briefly, then transfer the mixture to a food processor or a blender (in batches if needed) and puree.

Return the soup to the saucepan and add the coconut milk and ½ cup of the pistachios. Season with salt and pepper. Bring the soup to a simmer and cook for about 5 minutes, then serve with the remaining ¼ cup pistachios on top.

IMPROVEMENT: Thin the soup a bit with additional broth; also, it's delicious served cold.

Eggplant "caviar" is essentially eggplant that's roasted until it nearly collapses and the interior turns into a creamy puree that can be seasoned at will. Salt and pepper, olive oil, and lemon juice are typical additions. Add tahini and this turns into Middle Eastern baba ganoush. This recipe, from the *LVIS Centennial Cookbook*, is unusual for including tomato, which is not traditional, for extra enrichment.

SERVES 8

Poor Man's Caviar
NATASHA LARY

1 LARGE EGGPLANT, ABOUT 1½ POUNDS

4 TABLESPOONS EXTRA VIRGIN OLIVE OIL

½ CUP MINCED ONION

3 CLOVES GARLIC, MINCED

¼ CUP TOMATO PUREE

1 TEASPOON LEMON JUICE

SALT AND FRESHLY GROUND BLACK PEPPER

PITTED BLACK OLIVES FOR GARNISH

BLACK BREAD OR PITA CHIPS FOR SERVING

Preheat the oven to 375°F.

Place the eggplant in a shallow baking dish and roast for 40 minutes, or until tender when pierced with a knife. Remove from the oven and let cool. Cut the eggplant in half vertically and scoop out the flesh into a bowl.

Meanwhile, heat 1 tablespoon of the olive oil in a large skillet over low heat. Add the onion and sauté until translucent, about 2 minutes. Add the garlic and sauté for another minute. Remove from the heat. Add the eggplant flesh to the skillet along with the tomato puree. Bring to a simmer and cook for 15 minutes, stirring, and gradually adding the remaining olive oil, until the ingredients are well blended and thick. Stir in the lemon juice and season with salt and pepper.

Transfer to a serving dish, garnish with olives around or on top of the mixture, and chill for at least 2 hours. Serve with black bread or pita chips.

IMPROVEMENT: Grill the eggplant, turning it frequently, until it is soft, to give your "caviar" a hauntingly smoky flavor. Another variation is to omit the tomato and onion and simply fold some pesto (page 54) into the roasted eggplant puree.

Christie's Couscous

CHRISTIE BRINKLEY

6 TABLESPOONS EXTRA VIRGIN OLIVE OIL

2½ TABLESPOONS BALSAMIC VINEGAR

JUICE OF ½ LEMON

1 TEASPOON DRY MUSTARD

SALT AND FRESHLY GROUND BLACK PEPPER

2⅓ CUPS VEGETABLE BROTH

1½ CUPS INSTANT COUSCOUS

½ CUP ENGLISH PEAS, FRESH OR FROZEN

1 CUP FRESH CORN KERNELS, CUT FROM 2 EARS OF CORN

1 MEDIUM ZUCCHINI, CUT INTO 1-INCH PIECES

1 SMALL RED BELL PEPPER, CORED AND DICED

1 (15-OUNCE) CAN CHICKPEAS, DRAINED, RINSED, AND DRAINED AGAIN

¼ CUP FRESH MINT LEAVES, COARSELY CHOPPED

In a small bowl, whisk together 4 tablespoons of the oil, the vinegar, lemon juice, and mustard. Season with salt and pepper and set aside.

Place the broth in a 2-quart saucepan. Add the remaining 2 tablespoons oil and ½ teaspoon salt. Bring to a boil and slowly add the couscous. Stir. Cover the pot and remove it from the heat. Let stand for 5 minutes, or until the liquid has been absorbed. Fluff the couscous with a fork, then transfer it to a large serving bowl.

Place the peas in a saucepan, cover with water, and bring to a boil. Reduce the heat to low and simmer until tender, about 5 minutes. Add the corn and zucchini, simmer just another minute or so, then drain the vegetables and fold into the couscous. Fold in the red pepper, chickpeas, and mint. Whisk the dressing again, pour it over the couscous, and combine all the ingredients well.

IMPROVEMENT: For a different presentation, keep the couscous and vegetables separate and divide the dressing between the two, then pack the plain couscous into a bowl, unmold it onto a platter, and surround it with the vegetables.

In the *LVIS Centennial Cookbook*, the supermodel Christie Brinkley pointed out that this couscous salad was a vegetarian recipe. She also suggested adding vegetables other than the ones she specified, which accounts for the zucchini in the mix. Chunks of cooked sweet potatoes, carrots, or eggplant could be included, especially if the season does not provide items like fresh corn.

SERVES 6

Moroccan Carrot Salad

KATIE LEE

3 LARGE CARROTS, PEELED AND VERY THINLY SLICED ON AN ANGLE

SALT

1 TEASPOON GROUND CUMIN

½ TEASPOON SWEET PAPRIKA

PINCH OF GROUND CINNAMON

PINCH OF CAYENNE

2 TABLESPOONS EXTRA VIRGIN OLIVE OIL

GRATED ZEST AND JUICE OF 1 LEMON

1 SMALL CLOVE GARLIC, MINCED

¼ CUP PACKED FLAT-LEAF PARSLEY LEAVES, CHOPPED

¼ CUP PACKED FRESH MINT LEAVES, CHOPPED

FRESHLY GROUND BLACK PEPPER

Place the carrot slices in a 2-quart saucepan, cover with water, and add ½ teaspoon salt. Bring to a boil and cook for 1 minute. Drain well, then pat the slices dry with a paper towel. Put the carrots in a bowl that will hold them with room to spare.

Place the cumin, paprika, cinnamon, and cayenne in a small dry skillet. Cook over medium-low heat, stirring, until the spices start to turn fragrant, about 1 minute. Add the oil, swirl the pan, then add the lemon zest and juice and garlic. Cook for about 30 seconds, stirring. Remove from the heat, pour over the carrots, stir with a spatula, and set aside to cool to room temperature. Fold in the parsley and mint, season with salt and pepper, stir to combine, and set aside to marinate for at least 2 hours or overnight before serving.

IMPROVEMENT: Use multicolored carrots—white, yellow, orange, red, and purple. They're widely available.

Katie Lee, a television celebrity cook, is devoted to the Hamptons and draws culinary inspiration from what she finds at farm stands and in markets. This salad is one of those recipes that only improves a day or two after it's made. A carrot salad like this one is a typical addition to the array of appetizers served at a Moroccan dinner.

SERVES 4

I have gathered mussels from jetties and beaches. These days, the ones that are sold in fish markets are usually farm-raised in Canada and are much cleaner. But wild Long Island mussels, when they're available under the right weather and water quality conditions, tend to have a brinier flavor. This preparation is from Rowdy Hall, a restaurant owned by the group whose flagship is Nick & Toni's.

SERVES 2 TO 4

Steamed Mussels
ROWDY HALL

3 TABLESPOONS EXTRA VIRGIN OLIVE OIL

¾ CUP THINLY SLICED SHALLOTS

2 TABLESPOONS MINCED GARLIC

2 POUNDS MUSSELS, SCRUBBED AND DEBEARDED

¾ CUP DRY WHITE WINE

½ CUP HEAVY CREAM

3 TABLESPOONS MINCED FLAT-LEAF PARSLEY LEAVES

SALT AND FRESHLY GROUND BLACK PEPPER

CRUSTY BREAD FOR SERVING

Place a large sauté pan or casserole over medium-high heat. Add the oil, and when it is hot, add the shallots and garlic. Cook until softened but not browned, about 1 minute. Add the mussels and wine and cook for 2 minutes. Stir in the cream. Cover the pan, leaving the lid slightly ajar, and cook until the mussels open, about 5 minutes. Discard any mussels that do not open.

Strew with the parsley. Taste the broth and season with salt and pepper as needed. Divide the mussels and sauce among shallow bowls and serve with crusty bread for sopping.

IMPROVEMENT: This basic preparation welcomes variations, like using littleneck clams in addition to the mussels or sizzling some chorizo slices or other sausage along with the shallots. Be sure to have an empty bowl on the table for discarded mussel shells.

Rosemary-Roasted Striped Bass

NANCY SKURNIK

2 LARGE BUNCHES FRESH ROSEMARY

1 LARGE RED ONION, THINLY SLICED

1 (2-POUND) CENTER-CUT FILLET WILD STRIPED BASS, HALIBUT,
    OR ALASKAN SALMON, ALL WITH SKIN

SALT AND FRESHLY GROUND BLACK PEPPER

2 LARGE LEMONS, THINLY SLICED AND SEEDED

⅓ CUP EXTRA VIRGIN OLIVE OIL

Spread one bunch of the rosemary in a single layer in the bottom of a baking pan that can hold the fish comfortably. Spread the onion slices over the rosemary. Place the fish, skin-side down, on top. Season with salt and pepper. Spread the second bunch of rosemary on the fish and top with the lemon slices, arranged in a row. Drizzle the olive oil over all. Cover and refrigerate for up to 4 hours if not planning to cook immediately. Let it come to room temperature, about 30 minutes, before roasting.

Preheat the oven to 500°F.

Roast the fish for 20 minutes, or until just done (opaque in the middle); if using salmon, you may wish to reduce the cooking time to 12 to 15 minutes for medium-rare to medium. Using a large spatula, transfer the fish to a warm platter along with the rosemary, onion, and lemon, and serve.

IMPROVEMENT: Regardless of which of the recommended fish you use, you will want to extract the pin bones. You'll find them by placing the fillet skin side down and lightly running your hand over the flesh. You'll notice little tips of bones sticking out. A needle-nose pliers from the hardware store is the best tool for yanking them out. I keep a pair in a kitchen drawer to use only for this purpose.

This handsome and delicious preparation, from an LVIS member, was designed for a salmon fillet. But since salmon is not a local fish, it is worthwhile to try options from Long Island waters. Most notably our monarch of fishes, the meaty and delectable wild striped bass, which runs from summer through fall, would suit this menu. Local halibut is another option. Both of these fish should be cooked just until the flesh turns opaque, not more. And if you insist on salmon, look for seasonal Alaskan wild king (Chinook) or sockeye, not farmed Atlantic salmon.

SERVES 4

Once the seasonal tomato crop is gone, it's gone. But before that, it does linger on, well into fall. It's fun to gather an array of these local beauties in various sizes and colors and toss them together in a kaleidoscope of salad, simply dressed with good olive oil, sea salt, and pepper.

SERVES 4

Tomato Finale
FLORENCE FABRICANT

½ CUP PINE NUTS

2 POUNDS ASSORTED TOMATOES, SUCH AS CHERRY, SMALL HEIRLOOM, AND PLUM, IN MIXED COLORS

3 TABLESPOONS FRUITY EXTRA VIRGIN OLIVE OIL

ZEST OF 1 LEMON

COARSE SEA SALT AND FRESHLY GROUND BLACK PEPPER

Toast the pine nuts in a small dry skillet over medium heat, stirring so they cook evenly, about 5 minutes. Remove from the pan and set aside.

Halve the cherry tomatoes. Core the other varieties and cut them into 1½-inch pieces. Place them all in a shallow bowl. Add the olive oil and lemon zest and gently mix. Spread them in a serving dish, season with salt and pepper, and scatter the pine nuts on top.

Dreesen's, once a fixture on East Hampton's Newtown Lane, was a butcher shop and grocery that was owned by several generations of the DeSanti family. Today their famous cake doughnuts—plain, cinnamon-sugared, or in a drift of powdered sugar—live on, sold at the ice cream shop that now occupies the old storefront. Inevitably, you buy too many. Not to worry. Dreesen's uses its leftovers for an easy bread pudding, which was published in the *LVIS Centennial Cookbook*, and so can you.

SERVES 4 TO 6

Doughnut Pudding
DREESEN'S MARKET

¾ CUP WHOLE MILK

3 LARGE EGGS

½ CUP SUGAR (REDUCE THE SUGAR TO ⅓ CUP IF USING
   CINNAMON-SUGAR DOUGHNUTS)

1 TEASPOON VANILLA EXTRACT

5 STALE PLAIN OR CINNAMON-SUGAR CAKE DOUGHNUTS,
   COARSELY CHOPPED

3 TABLESPOONS DRIED CURRANTS

3 TABLESPOONS UNSALTED BUTTER

1 TEASPOON GROUND CINNAMON

ICE CREAM, PREFERABLY COFFEE, FOR SERVING

In a medium bowl, beat the milk and eggs together until well blended. Beat in the sugar, then stir in the vanilla. Add the doughnut pieces and mix well. Add the currants. Let sit for 15 minutes so the doughnuts soak up the milk and egg mixture.

Preheat the oven to 350°F. Use 1 tablespoon of the butter to grease an 8-inch square or round baking dish, preferably one that you'd bring to the table.

Spread the doughnut mixture in the prepared baking dish. Dot with the remaining butter and sprinkle with the cinnamon.

Place in the oven and bake for 45 minutes to 1 hour, until the top is crusty and browned. Allow to cool for at least 20 minutes, then serve with ice cream on the side.

IMPROVEMENTS: OK, the ice cream does not have to be coffee, but what's better than coffee and doughnuts?

OUR OWN
ZUCHINI
$2.50/lb

OUR
Beets 3.00/bunch

OUR
RADISHES
$3/bunch

OUR
SPINACH
$3.50

Round Swamp Farm

SNYDER

LIVE
LOBSTERS!

FRESH FISH
SWEET CORN
STRAWBERRIES
BLUEBERRIES

PIKE FARMS

HARVEST SEASON

The growing season on the South Fork of Long
Island extends into fall. The seas, which maintain
chilly air in spring and give the local agriculture a
late start, moderate the temperature once summer
has passed on the calendar. That's why local
vineyards can ripen red grapes and you just might
have local corn at Thanksgiving. This menu makes
the most of the season, of the produce that lingers
beyond summer, and of perennial seafood.
Beer from a local brewery, a rich local chardonnay,
or a young merlot will suit this menu.

Zucchini-Sausage Quiche • Sea Scallops over Corn Relish
Sunflower Seed Salad • Fruit Crisp

Having a quiche in one's repertoire is essential. It can provide hors d'oeuvres, a first course, a main course, and, without the cheese but with sufficient sweetening or fruit, a custard tart for dessert. Through early fall in the Hamptons, zucchini are still abundant. This LVIS member's recipe exploits them before they're gone.

SERVES 6

Zucchini-Sausage Quiche
NANCY ERDOS

PASTRY FOR 9-INCH TART (RECIPE FOLLOWS)

ALL-PURPOSE FLOUR FOR THE WORK SURFACE

4 TABLESPOONS UNSALTED BUTTER

2 CUPS SHREDDED ZUCCHINI (FROM ABOUT 3 SMALL ZUCCHINI)

2 LINKS (8 OUNCES) SWEET ITALIAN SAUSAGE, CASINGS REMOVED, CRUMBLED

1 CUP SHREDDED GRUYÈRE CHEESE

4 LARGE EGGS

1½ CUPS HALF-AND-HALF

SALT AND FRESHLY GROUND BLACK PEPPER

¼ CUP GRATED PARMIGIANO-REGGIANO

Prepare the pastry.

Preheat the oven to 450°F.

Roll the pastry into a 12-inch circle on a lightly floured surface. Line a 9-inch tart pan with the pastry, trim the edges, line with foil, and fill with pastry weights or dry beans. Bake for about 8 minutes, until the pastry looks dry. Remove from the oven, remove the foil and weights, and set aside to cool. Leave the oven on.

Melt 2 tablespoons of the butter in a skillet. Add the zucchini and sauté for about 2 minutes, until wilted. Spread the zucchini in the tart shell.

Melt the remaining 2 tablespoons butter in the skillet over medium heat. Add the sausage pieces to the skillet and cook, stirring and crushing with a fork, until the sausage becomes uniformly textured and has lost its pink color, about 5 minutes. Meanwhile, line a dish with a paper towel. Transfer the sausage to the paper towel to drain, then add it to the tart shell. Scatter the Gruyère cheese on top.

Beat the eggs in a medium bowl, stir in the half-and-half, and season with salt and pepper. Pour the egg mixture into the tart shell. Dust with the Parmesan cheese.

Bake for 10 minutes, lower the oven temperature to 350°F, and bake for another 30 minutes or so, until the filling feels firm. Remove from the oven, let cool for 15 to 20 minutes, then serve.

PASTRY

MAKES ONE 9-INCH TART SHELL

1½ CUPS ALL-PURPOSE FLOUR, PLUS EXTRA FOR ROLLING

½ TEASPOON SALT

4 OUNCES (1 STICK) COLD UNSALTED BUTTER, CUT INTO ½-INCH PIECES

1 LARGE EGG YOLK

4 TABLESPOONS COLD WATER, PLUS MORE IF NEEDED

Place the flour and salt in a food processor. Pulse briefly to mix. Add the butter and pulse about 15 times, until the mixture is uniformly crumbly.

In a small bowl, beat the egg yolk with the cold water. Sprinkle over the flour mixture in the food processor and pulse until the mixture starts to come together. Add a little more water if needed. Gather the dough into a ball, place it on a lightly floured work surface, and form it into a smooth disc. Wrap it in plastic and refrigerate for 30 minutes.

IMPROVEMENT: Though the recipe calls for sweet Italian sausage, it is also excellent when made with a mixture of sweet and hot sausage, crumbled cooked bacon, or chorizo. And for non-meat eaters, diced smoked seafood is an option.

Though Peconic Bay scallops are the pride of the East End of Long Island, the larger meaty sea scallops are harvested year-round. This recipe from an LVIS member pairs the sea scallops with fresh corn, which is still picked in the fields and stacked at farm stands well into October.

SERVES 6

Sea Scallops over Corn Relish

AIMEE DALLOB

3 TABLESPOONS EXTRA VIRGIN OLIVE OIL

2 TABLESPOONS FINELY DICED SHALLOT

3 TABLESPOONS FINELY DICED RED BELL PEPPER

KERNELS FROM 5 EARS OF FRESH YELLOW OR BI-COLOR CORN

10 RED OR YELLOW GRAPE TOMATOES, HALVED

SALT AND FRESHLY GROUND BLACK PEPPER

2 TABLESPOONS UNSALTED BUTTER

2 POUNDS SEA SCALLOPS, SIDE TENDONS REMOVED, PATTED DRY

Heat 2 tablespoons of the olive oil in a large skillet, preferably nonstick, over medium heat. Add the shallots and bell pepper and sauté until starting to soften, about 3 minutes. Add the corn, raise the heat to medium-high, and sauté for about 5 minutes, long enough to cook the corn. Add the tomatoes and cook for another minute or so, until starting to soften. Season with salt and pepper. Spread on a serving platter and cover with foil to keep warm.

Add the remaining 1 tablespoon oil and the butter to the skillet and heat over medium until the butter is melted and the pan is hot. Season the scallops with salt and pepper and add them in a single layer to the skillet. (If necessary, you can brown the scallops in two batches.) Sear for 2 to 3 minutes without disturbing, until lightly browned on one side. Turn the scallops and cook the second side for about 2 minutes, until lightly browned. Arrange the scallops on the corn mixture and serve, or keep tented with foil to serve within an hour; the dish does not need to be piping hot.

IMPROVEMENT: The corn ragout can be called upon to do much more than embellish seared scallops. It will hold its own as a side dish, can enrich a soup, or be added to a salad.

Sunflower Seed Salad

FLORENCE FABRICANT

1½ TABLESPOONS ROASTED UNSALTED SUNFLOWER SEEDS

1 TABLESPOON APPLE CIDER VINEGAR

2 TABLESPOONS COLD-PRESSED SUNFLOWER OIL OR PUMPKIN SEED OIL

30 YELLOW GRAPE TOMATOES, HALVED

1 MEDIUM HEAD LEAF LETTUCE, PREFERABLY PURPLE, TORN INTO
   BITE-SIZE PIECES

SALT AND FRESHLY GROUND BLACK PEPPER

Place the sunflower seeds in a small skillet over medium-high heat. Toast them, stirring, until they are lightly browned, about 5 minutes. Place in a salad bowl. Add the vinegar, oil, and tomatoes. Stir and set aside for at least 15 minutes.

Just before serving, add the lettuce. Toss, season with salt and pepper, and serve.

Just one giant sunflower in a slender vase will brighten a room. And a field of them is a late summer joy to behold as one drives along the roads and lanes within view of the sea. This salad is a colorful homage to sunflowers, using the seeds and the nutty oil to mix with baby tomatoes and sultry dark lettuce leaves.

SERVES 6

East Hampton has a storied literary heritage, with a long list of prominent writers among its residents. Philip Schultz, the Pulitzer Prize-winning poet, is one of them. Though he contributed this recipe, when I chatted with him about it at a dinner party, he demurred at calling it his own. He preferred to credit his wife, Monica Banks, a sculptor, with this sensational dessert.

SERVES 6 TO 8

Fruit Crisp
PHILIP SCHULTZ AND MONICA BANKS

4 OUNCES (1 STICK) UNSALTED BUTTER, SOFTENED

4 CUPS PEELED PITTED FRUIT CUT INTO SLICES OR CHUNKS

JUICE OF 1 LEMON

½ TEASPOON GROUND CINNAMON

½ CUP GRANULATED SUGAR

½ CUP PACKED LIGHT BROWN SUGAR

1 TEASPOON GRATED LEMON ZEST

PINCH OF SALT

1 CUP ALL-PURPOSE FLOUR

WHIPPED CREAM OR ICE CREAM FOR SERVING

Use a little of the butter to grease a 9-inch glass pie dish or cast-iron skillet.

Mix the fruit with the lemon juice and a pinch of the cinnamon in a medium bowl and spread it in the pie dish.

Mix both of the sugars, the remaining cinnamon, the lemon zest, salt, and flour in a large bowl. Add the remaining butter in pieces and, using your fingertips, a large fork, two knives, or a pastry blender, mix the ingredients together until they are crumbly. Do not shortchange the mixing; it may take longer than you expect to achieve a uniform texture.

Spread the crumb mixture over the fruit, place in the oven, and bake until the topping starts to brown, 45 minutes to 1 hour. Remove from the oven and allow to cool to room temperature.

Serve with whipped cream or ice cream on the side.

IMPROVEMENT: By early fall ripe peaches may still beckon, plums will still be available, and apples and pears will be ready. Any of these fruits will suit this recipe.

HOME AFTER
the MOVIES

Jaws put a fictionalized East End on movie screens.
But the film world has had a long and interesting
history in the East Hampton area. Local lore has it
that scenes from the 1921 film *The Sheik* with Rudolph
Valentino were shot in an area of high dunes, called
the Walking Dunes, just west of Montauk. The beloved
Sag Harbor Cinema, recently restored after a fire,
was originally built in 1919. The increasingly important
Hamptons International Film Festival, a fall event, is
scheduled on screens throughout the area and, in
the off-season, shows films at Guild Hall, the cultural
center of East Hampton. And, of course, among the
residents of the Hamptons are film stars, writers,
directors, and producers galore. Going to the movies
also raises the question of where to eat. With a little
advance preparation, dinner at home becomes a genial
option. This menu shows the way. A rich white wine or
a light red will complement it.

Tuscan White Bean Soup with Kale
Monkfish with Lemon and Capers • Beet Salad
Caramel Baked Pears • Brittany Cake

Nick & Toni's is the magnet restaurant in East Hampton. In business since 1988, it still draws a crowd year-round; high-profile, regulars, and visitors. Many of chef Joe Realmuto's recipes, like this one, depend on the harvest from the restaurant's own garden or crops from nearby farms. To prepare the salad in advance, even early in the day, complete the recipe up to the point where you'd mix the beets and watercress with the dressing.

SERVES 4 TO 6

Beet Salad
JOE REALMUTO, NICK & TONI'S

RED WINE VINAIGRETTE (RECIPE FOLLOWS)
16 BABY RED BEETS (ABOUT 2 BUNCHES), OR 4 REGULAR BEETS
8 BABY YELLOW BEETS (ABOUT 1 BUNCH), OR 2 REGULAR YELLOW BEETS
½ CUP SHELLED UNSALTED PISTACHIOS
6 OUNCES PLAIN SOFT GOAT CHEESE, AT ROOM TEMPERATURE
¼ CUP HEAVY CREAM
SALT AND FRESHLY GROUND BLACK PEPPER
1 CUP BABY WATERCRESS LEAVES OR MÂCHE

Prepare the red wine vinaigrette.

Preheat the oven to 375°F.

Scrub the beets and trim the stems flush with the bulbs. Place the red and yellow beets in separate baking pans. Add 1 cup of water to the red beets and ½ cup water to the yellow beets. Cover the baking pans with foil and roast for 45 minutes to 1 hour, until the beets are tender when pierced with a paring knife. While the beets are roasting, spread the pistachios in a baking pan and toast them in the oven for about 8 minutes, until lightly browned. Remove and let cool, then chop them.

Remove the beets from the oven and let cool until they can be handled. Use paper towels to rub off their skins. Cut the baby beets in half. If using regular beets, cut each quarter in half. Refrigerate the beets.

Mash the goat cheese in a small bowl. Add the cream and work it in to make a smooth puree. Season with salt and pepper. Set aside.

To serve, place the beets in a large bowl with the watercress. Add about one-third of the vinaigrette dressing and toss. Adjust the amount of dressing to your liking. Divide the goat cheese mixture and place in the center of each of four to six salad plates and use the back of the spoon to spread it in a circle. Place the beets and watercress on top of the goat cheese, sprinkle with pistachios, and serve.

RED WINE VINAIGRETTE

1 SMALL SHALLOT, QUARTERED

¼ CUP RED WINE VINEGAR

1½ TABLESPOONS HONEY

1 TABLESPOON DIJON MUSTARD

¾ CUP EXTRA VIRGIN OLIVE OIL

SALT AND FRESHLY GROUND BLACK PEPPER

Turn on a food processor. Drop the shallot through the feed tube to mince it. Stop the machine, scrape down the sides, and add the vinegar, honey, and mustard. Turn on the machine and process for about 30 seconds, until the ingredients are finely blended. With the machine running, slowly pour in the oil. Season the dressing with salt and pepper. Set aside.

IMPROVEMENT: Other root vegetables, including carrots or turnips, can replace the beets in this salad.

You probably will have more dressing than the opposite recipe requires; refrigerate the rest for another salad.

MAKES 1⅓ CUPS

Caramel Baked Pears

CAROL McCALLION

6 RIPE BUT FIRM BOSC PEARS

1 TABLESPOON LEMON JUICE

1 CUP PACKED LIGHT BROWN SUGAR

3 TABLESPOONS UNSALTED BUTTER

VANILLA ICE CREAM FOR SERVING

Preheat the oven to 350°F.

Halve and core the pears. Arrange them cut-side up in a baking dish that will hold them in a single layer. Brush with the lemon juice.

Combine the brown sugar and butter in a small saucepan. Add ⅔ cup water, stir, and place over medium heat. Bring to a boil, then reduce the heat and simmer, stirring from time to time, for about 5 minutes, until the mixture has thickened. Brush this caramel on the pears. Cover the dish loosely with foil and bake for 10 minutes. Remove the foil and bake for another 15 minutes or so, basting once or twice, until the pears are tender.

Remove from the oven, baste again, and let cool for at least 1 hour. Baste again. Place two pear halves on each of six plates and top each with a scoop of ice cream. Spoon any additional caramel sauce from the baking dish over the ice cream and serve.

IMPROVEMENT: This recipe was designed for firm-textured Bosc pears. But ripe Asian pears or even apples can be substituted, though they require up to 15 minutes longer to bake before the foil is removed.

This recipe from an LVIS member is easily completed in advance and is one of the attractions in the *LVIS Centennial Cookbook*.

SERVES 6

As the chairperson of the cake and jam booth at the LVIS Fair, this member knows baking. A personal favorite is this French cake, also called gâteau Breton, from a recipe she obtained about forty years ago from a friend, Mimi Boleis, who came from Quiberon in Brittany, France. It's a simple almond-scented confection that can be made entirely by hand, as a French housewife might years ago, but is easier by machine. The texture is fairly dense yet tender. The cake is excellent to serve with local strawberries or other fruit, or as for this menu, alongside pears baked in caramel.

SERVES 8

Brittany Cake
JENNIFER MULLIGAN

3 CUPS ALL-PURPOSE FLOUR

1½ TEASPOONS BAKING POWDER

¼ TEASPOON SALT

8 OUNCES (2 STICKS) UNSALTED BUTTER, SOFTENED

1 CUP SUGAR

6 LARGE EGG YOLKS

1 TABLESPOON ALMOND EXTRACT

1 LARGE EGG WHITE

Preheat the oven to 350°F.

Whisk together the flour, baking powder, and salt in a large bowl. Set aside. By machine, preferably a stand mixer, beat the butter and sugar together on medium speed until creamy. Beat in the egg yolks one at a time. Beat in the almond extract. On low speed, beat in the flour mixture in four additions, making sure it's well blended at the end. The result will be a very soft dough.

Press the dough into a 9-inch tart pan, preferably with a removable bottom. Use a fork to trace a geometric pattern of lines in the top surface. In a small bowl, beat the egg white with 1 tablespoon water and brush on top of the cake.

Place in the oven and bake for 40 minutes, or until the top is golden brown and a cake tester or toothpick comes out clean. Let cool on a rack for 30 minutes. Remove the sides, then the bottom of the pan, and let cool completely. Transfer to a serving plate.

IMPROVEMENT: Scatter 3 tablespoons sliced almonds on top of the cake before baking.

LEAF-RAKING LUNCH

Does anyone rake leaves anymore, or have leaf
blowers completely taken over? On a bright fall
day, for this menu, leaf-raking is simply a metaphor
for an outdoor activity when the air is clear and
crisp and everything around is golden and amber.
Pumpkin-picking? Firewood-gathering? Walking
on the beach? All good and appetite-whetting.
Consider pouring glasses of chilled local cider,
alcoholic or not, with this lunch.

East End Clam Pie • Brussels Caesar Salad
Apples and Cheeses

Apples and Cheeses

Apples peak in October. Many varieties are grown, but for those in the know, the premier eating apple is the tart-sweet, often small Macoun. You won't find them in supermarkets. They're best enjoyed out of hand, not for cooking. And the harvest is limited. Buy them early in the season.

As for cheeses to accompany your apples, the premier producer on the South Fork is Mccox Bay Dairy, on a farm dating from 1875 near the sea in Bridgehampton. There, Art Ludlow and his sons, Pete and John, tend Jersey cows and produce an increasingly diverse array of artisanal cheeses. They make a farmhouse cheddar, an alpine-style cheese sold both young and aged, a blue cheese, a soft-ripening Camembert-style, a stinky washed-rind variety, and ricotta. They are unique in the area. Up on the North Fork goat cheeses and some cow's milk cheeses are made. Fresh handmade mozzarella is available throughout the region.

ITALIAN NIGHT

When it comes to appealing menus, Italian is always a good bet. Italian restaurants, from pizza places to high-end establishments, are in good supply in East Hampton, as are the ingredients a cook requires to put an Italian menu on the table. This dinner makes its debut with a classic: linguine dressed with briny local littleneck clams. A meat loaf with an Italian cheese-and-tomato twist, made from turkey, will follow, with a mellow dish of sautéed fennel alongside. For dessert there's cheesecake, not a ricotta-based Italian confection, but a cheesecake along the lines of New York style, only lighter. What gives it a touch of Italy is the crust made from biscotti, not the usual graham cracker crumbs. Only a few Italian varietals are being cultivated for wine on Long Island, but Channing Daughters, a South Fork winery, grows an array of atypical grapes, including pinot grigio, which it makes into a wine that has real character, unlike many Italian imports.

Linguine with Clams • Napeague Turkey Loaf
Braised Fennel with Golden Raisins • Italian-ish Cheesecake

The basis for this recipe is fairly standard. For this book we were offered several, and the result depends on the cream cheese, sour cream, sugar, and eggs you'll find in most, though the proportions may differ somewhat. The author's variation, to give the dessert a touch of Italian flavor, calls for almond extract instead of vanilla and relies on almond biscotti crumbs, which you'll have to grind yourself.

SERVES 8 TO 12

Italian-ish Cheesecake
BOB SPINK

8 OUNCES ALMOND BISCOTTI

6 TABLESPOONS UNSALTED BUTTER

1 CUP PLUS 2 TABLESPOONS SUGAR

3 LARGE EGGS

24 OUNCES CREAM CHEESE, DICED

1 CUP SOUR CREAM

1 TEASPOON ALMOND EXTRACT

GRATED ZEST AND JUICE OF 1 LEMON

Preheat the oven to 400°F.

Break the biscotti in pieces and place in a food processor. Process until finely ground. Transfer to a bowl. Melt the butter in a small saucepan over medium heat until it starts to brown. Remove from the heat and add to the biscotti. Add 2 tablespoons of the sugar and mix well.

Line the bottom of a 9-inch springform pan with a circle of parchment paper. Press the crumb mixture into the bottom and partway up the sides of the pan. Place in the oven and bake for about 10 minutes, until lightly browned. Remove from the oven and set aside. Leave the oven on.

Using a stand mixer or handheld mixer, place the eggs in a bowl, beat lightly, and beat in the remaining 1 cup sugar until light and creamy. Beat in the cream cheese until very smooth. Beat in the sour cream, almond extract, and lemon zest and juice. Pour into the prepared crust and place in the oven. Lower the oven temperature to 350°F and bake for about 1 hour and 10 minutes, until the filling seems fairly firm. Turn off the oven and leave the cake in it for 45 minutes. Remove from the oven, let cool to room temperature, then refrigerate to chill for at least 4 hours before removing the sides and bottom of the pan.

IMPROVEMENT: For a bit of garnish, scatter toasted sliced almonds on top of the cake.

THANKSGIVING CLASSICS

East Hampton's Colonial atmosphere makes it an ideal setting for Thanksgiving. You can even find bogs in Napeague, just east of Amagansett, where wild cranberries flourish. And many of the farm stands remain open selling the last of the local produce as well as colorful winter squash, decorative gourds, and frilly ornamental kale. For many family gatherings in East Hampton, a sit-down dinner is a tradition. Others prefer potluck. Many years ago, Dallas Ernst, the widow of the artist Jimmy Ernst (whose father was the surrealist Max Ernst), would have a big Thanksgiving open house– potluck style–on the Saturday after the holiday. Here's a dinner menu, not potluck. After the punch bowl is drained, continue with a choice of red or white wines; either one will complement the turkey.

Bourbon Punch • Kabocha Squash Soup
Iacono Turkey • Baked Cheese Grits • Birdhouse Potatoes
with Brussels Sprouts, Snap Peas, and Mushrooms
Pumpkin Cake • Baked Apples

Bourbon Punch
JENNIFER GEORGES

8 CINNAMON STICKS
1 (750-MILLILITER) BOTTLE BOURBON
¼ CUP GINGER LIQUEUR
¼ CUP LEMON JUICE
½ CUP CRANBERRY JUICE
¾ CUP SUPERFINE SUGAR
BLOCK OF ICE FOR THE PUNCH BOWL
¾ CUP MADEIRA, PREFERABLY MALMSEY
24 OUNCES SPARKLING WATER
FRESHLY GRATED NUTMEG
FRESH CRANBERRIES FOR GARNISH

Lightly toast the cinnamon sticks by holding them with tongs over a flame or rolling them in a cast-iron skillet over high heat for a couple of minutes. Place them in a quart-size jar and pour the bourbon over them. Cover and set to steep overnight. Combine the ginger liqueur, lemon juice, and cranberry juice in a pitcher. Add the sugar and stir until it dissolves.

Strain the bourbon into a punch bowl over the block of ice. Stir the juice mixture, then stir in the Madeira and add to the punch bowl. Pour in the sparkling water and stir again for several minutes, until the mixture is chilled. Sprinkle on the nutmeg and float the cranberries on top. Serve in 3-ounce punch cups.

IMPROVEMENT: Consider using maple syrup in place of the sugar.

Kabocha Squash Soup
LOIS NESBITT

½ KABOCHA SQUASH OR OTHER WINTER SQUASH

5 CUPS CHICKEN STOCK OR VEGETABLE STOCK, PLUS MORE IF NEEDED

2 TABLESPOONS PUMPKIN SEED OIL OR EXTRA VIRGIN OLIVE OIL

2 TABLESPOONS PEELED AND FINELY MINCED FRESH GINGER

¼ CUP TAMARI OR OTHER SOY SAUCE

1 TEASPOON RICE WINE VINEGAR

1 TEASPOON GROUND CINNAMON

½ CUP HEAVY CREAM

½ TEASPOON CAYENNE

SALT

2 TABLESPOONS TOASTED PUMPKIN SEEDS

Preheat the oven to 400°F. Line a baking sheet with foil.

Scoop the seeds from the squash. Cut the squash into 2-inch chunks. You should have about 6 cups. Place on the prepared baking sheet and roast for 30 minutes, or until tender, turning the pieces once. Remove from the oven and peel off the skin. Place the squash in a food processor with 3 cups of the stock. Puree until smooth.

Heat the oil in a large saucepan over medium heat. Add the ginger and sauté until softened, about 5 minutes. Add the squash puree, the remaining 2 cups stock, the soy sauce, vinegar, and cinnamon. Bring to a simmer, then reduce the heat to low and cook for 30 minutes, stirring a few times. If the soup is getting too thick, add a little more stock. Stir in the cream and cayenne, season with salt, and simmer for 5 minutes longer. The consistency should be slightly thicker than heavy cream. Serve, with a sprinkling of pumpkin seeds on each bowl of soup.

IMPROVEMENT: You can omit the cream, but be sure the soup is not too thick; add more stock if needed. And consider serving either version in hollowed-out miniature pumpkins.

This LVIS member, an artist, specified kabocha squash, a plump, medium-size green- and/or red-skinned variety with orange flesh, for this soup. It's one of the gazillion colorful squashes that decorate farm stands in late fall and could even provide a centerpiece for the table. Other hard-skinned squashes and pumpkins can be substituted.

SERVES 6 TO 8

Iacono Turkey

Sal Iacono's chickens and eggs from the farm on the edge of East Hampton Village are local favorites. Sal is no longer with us, but the family keeps the farm going. In fall other birds, including Muscovy ducks, domestic turkeys, and sometimes lean wild turkeys, all dark meat, can be ordered. Whatever bird you choose, you can simply roast it according to the method you prefer, brining it first if you wish. For a regular turkey I prefer starting it upside-down on a V-shaped rack for about 30 minutes at 425°F to brown the underside, then turning it and estimating about 12 minutes per pound at 350°F, unstuffed. A wild turkey should be roasted at 325°F for about 15 minutes per pound. Roasting the bird unstuffed is easier; the stuffing or dressing can go alongside, baked in a casserole dish. Grits are included in this menu, so you could skip the stuffing altogether.

Baked Cheese Grits

SUE VAUGHAN

6 TABLESPOONS UNSALTED BUTTER, SOFTENED

7 CUPS CHICKEN STOCK

2 CUPS YELLOW STONE-GROUND GRITS

1 POUND SHARP WHITE CHEDDAR CHEESE, FINELY DICED

SALT AND FRESHLY GROUND BLACK PEPPER

4 LARGE EGGS, BEATEN

1 CUP GRATED ITALIAN PECORINO CHEESE

½ CUP MINCED FRESH CHIVES

Use a little of the butter to grease a 9 by 13-inch casserole dish.

Bring 6 cups of the stock to a simmer in a heavy 3-quart saucepan. Slowly pour in the grits in a thin stream, whisking constantly. Whisk until the grits are well mixed. Reduce the heat to low and simmer gently, stirring frequently with a wooden spoon, until the mixture is thick and smooth, about 10 minutes. Remove from the heat.

Preheat the oven to 350°F.

Stir the cheddar cheese into the grits until it has melted. Season with salt and pepper. Stir in the remaining 1 cup stock, the eggs, and the remaining butter until well blended. Pour into the baking dish, strew with the pecorino cheese, and bake for 35 to 40 minutes, until the top is lightly browned. Sprinkle with the chives and serve.

The grits can be prepared in advance and refrigerated. To reheat, bring the dish to room temperature and bake at 350°F for about 25 minutes.

IMPROVEMENT: Instead of the chives, you can top the casserole with a cup of freshly popped popcorn.

This LVIS member recommends this combination of grits and cheese as a brunch dish. That is certainly a fine idea. But it could also grace a Thanksgiving table; the reason was given in the *LVIS Centennial Cookbook*. In the early days of settlement and up to the early twentieth century, whole dried corn kernels with their outer husks removed, soaked and cooked for hours, were a Sunday dish on the East End. It could cook all day and did so while people went to church. Called samp, it was not unlike Mexican posole, which these days is far more popular. Samp was East Hampton's equivalent of Boston's baked beans. Cornmeal grits keep the corn tradition alive with a much easier preparation. Be sure to look for stone-ground cornmeal, grits, or polenta, preferably organic.

SERVES 8

Birdhouse Potatoes with Brussels Sprouts, Snap Peas, and Mushrooms

LAURIE ANDERSON

SALT

10 SMALL YUKON GOLD POTATOES

1 CUP SUGAR SNAP PEAS

1 PINT BRUSSELS SPROUTS (ABOUT 20), RINSED, TRIMMED, AND HALVED

1½ TABLESPOONS EXTRA VIRGIN OLIVE OIL

ZEST OF 1 LEMON

½ CUP MINCED SHALLOTS

4 OUNCES MEDIUM CREMINI MUSHROOMS, STEMMED AND QUARTERED

1¼ CUPS HEAVY CREAM OR HALF-AND-HALF

1 TABLESPOON DIJON MUSTARD

FRESHLY GROUND BLACK PEPPER

1 TABLESPOON FRESH THYME LEAVES

Bring a pot of water with ½ teaspoon salt to boil. Add the potatoes, reduce the heat to medium, and cook until tender, 10 to 12 minutes. Remove the potatoes and set them aside to cool. Add the peas to the pot, cook for 5 minutes, then drain them.

Toss the Brussels sprouts with 1½ teaspoons of the olive oil and the lemon zest and season with salt. Arrange them cut-side down in a large heavy skillet. Place over high heat, and when the Brussels sprouts start to sizzle, lower the heat to medium and cook for about 10 minutes, until lightly browned. Remove them from the pan. Add the shallots to the pan and cook until they have softened, about 5 minutes. Add the remaining oil. Stir in the mushrooms and cook until the mushrooms have wilted, another 5 minutes or so. Add the peas and cook briefly, stirring, until they have softened a bit, about 3 minutes. Quarter the potatoes and add them.

In a small bowl, whisk the cream and mustard together and add to the pan. Reduce the heat to low and cook, stirring, for about 5 minutes to slightly thicken the sauce. Season with salt and pepper. Transfer to a warm dish, scatter with the thyme, and serve.

Pumpkin Cake
BONNIE PIZZORNO

1 CUP GOLDEN RAISINS

1 CUP GRAPESEED OIL

3 CUPS ALL-PURPOSE FLOUR

2 TEASPOONS BAKING POWDER

2 TEASPOONS BAKING SODA

1 TEASPOON SALT

4 LARGE EGGS

1½ CUPS SUGAR

1 TEASPOON GROUND CINNAMON

1½ CUPS UNSWEETENED PUMPKIN PUREE

½ CUP COARSELY CHOPPED PECANS

Place the raisins in a bowl, cover with boiling water, and set aside.

Grease a 10-inch tube pan with a little of the oil.

In a medium bowl, whisk the flour, baking powder, baking soda, and salt together and set aside.

Place the eggs in the bowl of a stand mixer and beat on medium-high speed until they start to thicken and turn pale in color, about 5 minutes. Continue beating and gradually add the sugar. Beat in the cinnamon. Turn the machine to low speed and beat in the remaining oil and the pumpkin puree. Gradually beat in the flour mixture. Drain the raisins and fold them in, then fold in the pecans.

Scoop the batter into the baking pan and bake for about 1 hour, until a cake tester comes out clean. Let cool in the pan, then unmold and serve.

IMPROVEMENT: It's not pumpkin season? Use mashed ripe bananas (about 2) instead.

Pumpkin pie has its fans and its detractors. But no one will complain about this moist, delicious cake from the LVIS member who got this recipe from her hosts at a dinner party forty-five years ago and who bakes it to sell at the Fair. The original recipe called for raisins, which is how we suggest baking it; Pizzorno uses chopped dates. Take your pick. As for the pumpkin puree, the plain canned variety will be fine to use. But you might consider baking one of the many varieties of superb winter squash or pumpkins until tender and using the fresh puree. Farms in the Hamptons cultivate and sell a pale-skinned number called a cheese pumpkin, which is preferred, thanks to its dense flesh, for making cakes and pies.

SERVES 12

Talk about power couples. Eli Zabar, a son of Louis Zabar, who founded the iconic New York food emporium, has a market and restaurant empire of his own in Manhattan. For a few years, he and his wife, Devon Fredericks, whose first name has East Hampton written all over it, also ran the Amagansett Farmers Market. For her part, Fredericks was a founder of Loaves & Fishes in Sagaponack. Now Eli and Devon work together at the massive Eli's Manhattan and live part time in East Hampton, the South of France, and New York City. This recipe requires overnight preparation.

SERVES 4 TO 8

Baked Apples
ELI ZABAR AND DEVON FREDERICKS

2 CUPS MIXED DRIED FRUIT, CUT INTO SMALL PIECES (FIGS, PRUNES, AND APRICOTS WORK BEST; DON'T USE RAISINS OR CRANBERRIES)

1 CINNAMON STICK

1 WHOLE CLOVE

2 CUPS NONALCOHOLIC APPLE CIDER, WARMED

4 LARGE ROME APPLES

4 TABLESPOONS UNSALTED BUTTER

HEAVY CREAM, ICE CREAM, OR CRÈME FRAÎCHE FOR SERVING

Place the dried fruit in a bowl, add the cinnamon and clove, and cover with the cider. Set aside to steep overnight. It does not have to be refrigerated.

Preheat the oven to 325°F.

Slice off the top ¼ inch of each apple. Using a corer or a vegetable peeler, scoop out the core of each. Put 1 tablespoon of the butter in each cavity. Drain the soaked fruit, reserving the liquid. Place the apples in a baking dish that will hold them with a little room to spare, then pour ¼ cup of the liquid into the center of each apple. Add the remaining liquid around the apples. Pile the soaked fruit in the center and on top of each apple. Cover the baking dish with foil.

Bake the apples for 45 minutes. Uncover them and bake for another 30 minutes or so, occasionally basting them with the liquid, until the apples are very tender but still hold their shape. Remove from the oven and let cool to room temperature, 2 hours or so, or refrigerate and allow to come to room temperature before serving. The apples can be halved, vertically, for 8 servings at a large dinner. Serve with heavy cream, ice cream, or crème fraîche.

IMPROVEMENT: Adding some diced crystallized ginger to the dried fruit gives the apples a touch of heat.

WINTER DINNER PARTY

The demands of organizing a small dinner party
are different in winter than in summer. For the
menu, you can't rely on farm stand bounty.
A winter dinner might beg to be more gracious,
even dressier, than a casual summer affair.
Remember that you will need some place to put
coats. Heartier food should be on offer. And
lighting the oven is welcome. For this menu, the
herb topping for the oysters can be readied in
advance, as can the orange sauce for the duck, the
salad dressing, and the potato cakes, which can
be reheated when the duck comes out of the oven.
The dessert cake should be prepared the day
before. The dinner calls for a good red wine,
a South Fork reserve merlot or North Fork
cabernet franc, perhaps. Count on at least two
bottles, maybe three.

Isaac Newton Cocktail • Roast Oysters with Sorrel Sauce
Duck à l'Orange • Potato Cakes
Crunchy Iceberg Salad with Creamy Blue Cheese
Double Diabolo

It takes a long memory to identify the French chef who came to America to head his country's culinary team at the 1939 World's Fair in New York. Then World War II started and it was impossible for the group of French chefs to return home. So Soulé remained and opened a restaurant called Le Pavillon. Decades ago New York's French restaurants kept the tradition of closing for vacation in July or August and sometimes both. But rather than hang up his toque for the season, Soulé went east and became the chef at the Hedges Inn, a historic house at Town Pond. His recipe for duck à l'orange made with a whole duck appeared in the *LVIS Centennial Cookbook*. Here it's simplified, using only duck breasts, which are now readily available, and updated with the addition of miso as a thickener for the sauce.

SERVES 6

IMPROVEMENT: The sauce can be used with other meats, including roast pork, veal, chicken, or quail.

Duck à l'Orange
HENRI SOULÉ

2 ORANGES
2 TABLESPOONS SUGAR
½ CUP DUCK STOCK OR CHICKEN STOCK, WARMED
1 TABLESPOON RED MISO
2 BONELESS DUCK BREASTS (MAGRETS DE CANARD)
SALT AND FRESHLY GROUND BLACK PEPPER
¼ CUP COINTREAU

Cut the zest from the oranges in long, narrow strips and set aside. Cut off the pith down to the flesh and discard it. Remove the orange segments, cutting them out over a bowl to catch the juice, and reserve them. Place the zest in a small saucepan. Cover with water and simmer for 2 minutes. Strain and reserve the zest.

Place the sugar in a medium skillet with the juice from the oranges. Bring to a simmer over medium heat and cook until the mixture turns a light caramel, about 5 minutes. Remove from the heat and add the stock, but step back as you do so because the mixture may spatter. Stir to combine. Stir in the miso and the cooked orange zest and set aside.

Preheat the oven to 175°F.

Score the fat on the duck breasts in a crisscross pattern without cutting into the flesh. Season the duck on both sides with salt and pepper. Heat a cast-iron skillet large enough to hold the duck on high heat. Place the duck breasts skin-side down in the pan and sear just until the skin is beautifully bronzed, about 3 minutes. Turn the duck and place the pan in the oven for 1½ hours. The result will be medium-rare.

When the duck is done, remove it to a cutting board. Reheat the sauce over medium-low heat. Add the Cointreau and the reserved orange segments. Add a couple of spoonfuls of the duck fat and any duck juices from the cast-iron skillet. Season the sauce with salt and pepper.

Slice the duck breasts across the grain about ½-inch thick. Arrange on a platter. Spoon the sauce over the duck and serve.

Potato Cakes

JANET DAYTON

2 BAKING POTATOES, SCRUBBED

1 CUP ALL-PURPOSE FLOUR, PLUS MORE FOR SHAPING THE CAKES

1 TABLESPOON BAKING POWDER

½ TEASPOON SALT, OR MORE TO TASTE

2 TABLESPOONS UNSALTED BUTTER, SOFTENED

1 LARGE EGG, LIGHTLY BEATEN

GRAPESEED OIL OR UNSALTED BUTTER FOR FRYING

SOUR CREAM OR YOGURT AND FRESH CHIVES FOR SERVING (OPTIONAL)

Preheat the oven to 425°F.

Place the potatoes directly on the rack in the oven and bake for 45 minutes to 1 hour, until they are tender when pierced with a paring knife. Meanwhile, in a small bowl, whisk together the flour, baking powder, and salt and set aside.

When the potatoes are cool enough to handle, cut them in half lengthwise, scoop the flesh out into a bowl, and mash with the butter. Mix in the egg. Add the flour mixture and knead briefly until well blended. With floured hands, shape the mixture into 6 patties, or more or fewer, depending on your desired size. Refrigerate for at least 1 hour.

Pour enough oil into a large skillet to reach a depth of ¼ inch and heat over medium. Fry the potato cakes, turning once, until golden brown on both sides, about 5 minutes per side. Meanwhile, line a plate with paper towels. Drain the cakes briefly on the paper towels and serve. The cooked potato cakes can be held at room temperature for up to 3 hours, then reheated at 250°F for 15 to 20 minutes.

Serve with sour cream or yogurt and chives, if desired.

IMPROVEMENT: Make the cakes smaller and serve them topped with sour cream and caviar (trout or sturgeon) for a lovely first course.

These potato cakes, contributed by an LVIS member, elevate a simple baked potato to fine dining. They are easy to prepare and can be reheated.

SERVES 6

Crunchy Iceberg Salad with Creamy Blue Cheese
INA GARTEN

CREAMY BLUE CHEESE DRESSING

4 OUNCES ROQUEFORT CHEESE, CRUMBLED

⅔ CUP MAYONNAISE, HOMEMADE OR STORE-BOUGHT

⅓ CUP PLAIN GREEK YOGURT

1 TABLESPOON SHERRY VINEGAR

½ TEASPOON KOSHER SALT

¼ TEASPOON FRESHLY GROUND BLACK PEPPER

Place the cheese in a small microwave-safe bowl and microwave for 15 seconds, or until it begins to melt. Place the mayonnaise, yogurt, warm blue cheese, sherry vinegar, salt, and pepper in a food processor and process until smooth. Set aside or refrigerate until ready to use.

ICEBERG SALAD

4 TENDER INSIDE PARTS OF CELERY STALKS, TRIMMED AND SLICED CROSSWISE ¼ INCH THICK

6 ROUND RADISHES, TRIMMED AND THINLY SLICED

5 SCALLIONS, TRIMMED AND SLICED ¼ INCH THICK

1 HEAD ICEBERG LETTUCE, WILTED OUTER LEAVES REMOVED

6 OUNCES ROQUEFORT CHEESE, CRUMBLED

FLEUR DE SEL AND FRESHLY GROUND BLACK PEPPER

Combine the celery, radishes, and scallions in a bowl. Slice the head of lettuce crosswise to make 4 to 6 round disks that are ¾ inch thick. (The number of guests will determine the number of slices.) Place each on a large salad plate. Spoon the dressing on the lettuce and scatter the raw vegetables on top.

Scatter the crumbled cheese on and around the salad and season with fleur de sel and pepper. Serve.

A celebrity nationwide thanks to her television appearances and many cookbooks, Ina Garten is a full-time resident of East Hampton, where many of her broadcasts are produced. At one time she had a fancy food store, the Barefoot Contessa, on Newtown Lane, an establishment she originally founded in Westhampton but then moved. She contributed this recipe from her cookbook *Make It Ahead*.

SERVES 4 TO 6

IMPROVEMENT: This recipe makes about 1½ cups of the blue cheese dressing. This dressing can accommodate other lettuces, like Bibb, and also works as a dip.

The doyenne of entertaining and culinary style has a house on Lily Pond Lane in East Hampton and has long been a member of LVIS. This cake, an indulgent confection, is made the day before (and requires soaking the raisins two days before serving). Once baked and iced, it can keep for a few days more, assuming there is any left.

SERVES 10

Double Diabolo
MARTHA STEWART

½ CUP RAISINS

½ CUP SCOTCH WHISKEY

8 OUNCES (2 STICKS) UNSALTED BUTTER

9 TABLESPOONS CAKE FLOUR, PLUS MORE FOR THE PAN

22 OUNCES SEMISWEET CHOCOLATE, BROKEN INTO CHUNKS

6 LARGE EGGS, SEPARATED

1⅓ CUPS SUGAR

1⅓ CUPS GROUND ALMONDS (ALMOND FLOUR)

PINCH OF SALT

¾ TO 1 CUP HEAVY CREAM

Place the raisins in a dish, add the whiskey, and soak overnight.

Preheat the oven to 350°F. Use a little of the butter to grease a 12-inch cake pan (a 10-inch pan will also work, and the pan can be springform). Line the bottom with parchment and butter and flour the parchment.

Melt 14 ounces of the chocolate in a small saucepan or a double boiler. Add the butter little by little, stirring to keep the mixture smooth.

In a stand mixer, beat the egg yolks with the sugar until thick and creamy. Add the chocolate mixture on low speed. Fold in the cake flour and ground almonds. Stir in the raisins and whiskey.

In a clean mixer bowl, beat the egg whites with a pinch of salt until they hold peaks but are not dry. Fold the egg whites into the batter a third at a time. Spoon the batter into the cake pan, place in the oven, and bake for 25 minutes, or until a cake tester comes out fairly clean and the cake has started to shrink away from the sides of the pan. Remove from the oven and let sit for 10 minutes, then unmold the cake onto a wire rack to finish cooling. Peel off the parchment. Let cool completely.

For the frosting, melt the remaining 8 ounces of chocolate with ¾ cup of the cream in a small saucepan, whisking until smooth. Add up to ¼ cup more cream if needed for a creamy consistency. Pour over the cake and smooth with a spatula.

IMPROVEMENT: Accompany the cake with small snifters of good single malt.

HOLIDAY OPEN HOUSE

The local villages dress for the holidays. Small Christmas trees bedecked with colored lights line Main Street. Homes display festive wreaths and sparkle with decorations. The blades of the windmills are rimmed with strings of tiny bulbs and in East Hampton, a small tree lit with cobalt blue sits in the middle of Town Pond. To celebrate, an open house is often on the calendar. LVIS holds them in the stately house that is the group's headquarters for member families and for children. But here is an example of how to assemble a menu and game plan for a festive gathering at holiday time, most of which can be prepared in advance. And here are two final tips: be sure the dishwasher is empty before the doorbell rings, and put your coats on a bed, leaving the closet and hangers for guests.

White Star Punch • Benne Bits • Spanakopita
Chutney Cheese Spread • Cabbage Salad
Whole Roasted Cauliflower • Thai Red Seafood Curry
Double Jasmine Rice • Steak à la Stone with Mamie's Pepper Hash
Apricot Pecan Bars • Red Wine Cake (Rotweinkuchen)

In one corner of the sprawling Reutershan Parking Lot behind Main Street in East Hampton, the John Papas Cafe has been a reliable mealtime standby for decades. Diner "comfort food" from a grilled cheese sandwich to a burger or an omelet is served alongside a number of Greek specialties, among them this spinach pie.

MAKES 24 PIECES

IMPROVEMENT: The tip of deploying a potato ricer for extracting all the liquid from cooked or defrosted spinach can be used for other recipes.

Spanakopita
JOHN PAPAS CAFE

4 OUNCES (1 STICK) UNSALTED BUTTER, MELTED

2 TABLESPOONS EXTRA VIRGIN OLIVE OIL

1 CUP FINELY CHOPPED ONION

2 POUNDS FRESH BABY SPINACH (1 POUND FROZEN AND DEFROSTED SPINACH CAN BE SUBSTITUTED)

2 TABLESPOONS CHOPPED FRESH DILL

2 TABLESPOONS FRESHLY GROUND BLACK PEPPER

3 LARGE EGGS, BEATEN

6 OUNCES (¾ CUP) COTTAGE CHEESE OR RICOTTA CHEESE

7 OUNCES (1⅓ CUPS) CRUMBLED GREEK FETA CHEESE

SALT

8 OUNCES PHYLLO PASTRY, THAWED

Preheat the oven to 375°F. Brush an 8 by 12-inch baking dish with a little of the melted butter.

Heat the oil in a large skillet over medium heat. Add the onion and sauté until softened but not browned, about 2 minutes. Add the spinach (for frozen spinach, press it in a potato ricer to remove any liquid). Cook the spinach for about 5 minutes, until wilted and any liquid in the pan has evaporated. Remove the spinach to a cutting board and chop it fairly fine. Place in a large bowl. Add the dill, pepper, and eggs and mix well. Fold in the cheeses. Season with salt.

Unroll the phyllo onto a clean, damp dish towel on a work surface. Remove one sheet and cover the rest with the towel to keep moist. Line the prepared baking dish with the sheet of phyllo. Brush with a little of the melted butter. Repeat, using half the pastry sheets, but do not butter the top sheet. Spread the filling over the pastry. Then add another pastry sheet, butter it, and repeat until all the pastry sheets are used, brushing the top sheet with butter. Sprinkle a little water on top.

Use a very sharp knife to score the layers of pastry down to the filling in 2-inch squares. Bake for 40 minutes, or until golden brown. Allow to cool for at least 30 minutes, or let cool to room temperature. Cut the rest of the way through the scored lines to make squares for serving.

Like potatoes, cauliflower has long been a major crop on East End farms. In the fall there would be a cauliflower auction in Riverhead to set the price. It was discontinued in the 1980s, though the Long Island Cauliflower Association, which ran it, is still in business helping farmers. Most farms are more diversified now, or have planted vineyards where heads of cauliflower once sprouted, the leaves hand-tied over the florets to keep them white. But at the same time, cauliflower is riding a wave of popularity like never before, being used in new, delicious ways, even to make a grain-like substitute for rice. This recipe, from a Sag Harbor restaurant, involves roasting a whole head, one of the latest ways to prepare the vegetable. Guests can break off the florets and dip them in the sauce.

SERVES 6 OR MORE

Whole Roasted Cauliflower
LULU KITCHEN

1 MEDIUM HEAD CAULIFLOWER

SALT

3 TABLESPOONS EXTRA VIRGIN OLIVE OIL

FRESHLY GROUND BLACK PEPPER

½ TEASPOON ALEPPO PEPPER

½ TEASPOON SESAME SEEDS

1 CUP PLAIN GREEK YOGURT

1 CLOVE GARLIC, MASHED

JUICE OF 1 LEMON

Preheat the oven to 400°F.

Trim the leaves from the cauliflower and slice off any stem flush with the bottom of the head. Place the head in a large pot, cover three-quarters full with water, add 1 teaspoon salt, and bring to a boil. Reduce the heat to medium, cover, and cook for 15 minutes. Drain and place in a baking dish that can go to the table.

Brush the cauliflower with the oil and dust with salt, black pepper, and the Aleppo pepper. Sprinkle with the sesame seeds. Place in the oven and roast for 1 hour, or until the top of the cauliflower is nicely browned and very tender.

While the cauliflower is roasting, stir the yogurt in a small bowl to smooth it. In another small bowl, mix the garlic with the lemon juice, then mix it into the yogurt. Place in a small serving dish.

Serve the cauliflower with the sauce alongside for dipping and a couple of spoons so guests can pull pieces off.

IMPROVEMENT: Though this recipe calls for a yogurt-based sauce, other dips, like a soy-based Asian mixture, an aioli (page 89), or Caesar dressing (page 170) can be used.

For years, this delicious curry made at the reliable Seafood Shop in Wainscott has been a favorite of mine. It's an easy takeout lunch or supper item. I have even bought it to serve as the centerpiece for a New Year's Eve dinner. I was finally able to get the recipe for this book. How spicy you make it is a matter of taste, depending on the quantity of Thai red curry paste. As for the seafood, that can also be variable. Cooked mussels, pieces of lobster, and chunks of blackfish could be added. Aside from the monkfish and crabmeat, the choice of ingredients is up to you. The consistency is halfway between soup and stew.

SERVES 8 TO 12

Thai Red Seafood Curry
THE SEAFOOD SHOP

3 TABLESPOONS GRAPESEED OIL

1½ CUPS FINELY CHOPPED ONION

1 BUNCH SCALLIONS, FINELY CHOPPED

2 TABLESPOONS MINCED GARLIC

1 POUND WHITE MUSHROOMS, SLICED

¼ CUP SOY SAUCE

2 TO 3 TABLESPOONS FISH SAUCE, PREFERABLY THAI (NAM PLA)

42 OUNCES UNSWEETENED FULL-FAT COCONUT MILK (3 CANS)

3 OUNCES (¼ CUP) THAI RED CURRY PASTE

2 TABLESPOONS LIME JUICE

1 POUND MONKFISH, CUT INTO 1-INCH CHUNKS

1 POUND JUMBO LUMP CRABMEAT

8 LARGE SHRIMP, PEELED, DEVEINED, AND HALVED

8 OUNCES BAY SCALLOPS OR QUARTERED SEA SCALLOPS

3 TABLESPOONS MINCED FRESH CILANTRO LEAVES

Heat the oil in a large sauté pan over low heat. Add the onions and scallions and cook until they are translucent, about 2 minutes. Add the garlic and cook a few minutes more, until barely starting to color. Add the mushrooms and continue cooking, stirring occasionally, until the mushrooms soften, about 5 minutes. Stir in the soy sauce, fish sauce, and half the coconut milk. Bring to a simmer over low heat and cook for 10 minutes. Add half the red curry paste and the remaining coconut milk. Taste, then continue to add additional curry paste to taste. Add the lime juice. When the curry mixture is to your liking, cover and set aside.

About 20 minutes before serving, reheat the sauce over low heat. Add all of the seafood, cover, and cook for 10 to 15 minutes, until the seafood is cooked through. Transfer to a serving bowl or a tureen and garnish with the cilantro.

DOUBLE JASMINE RICE
FLORENCE FABRICANT

3 JASMINE TEA BAGS

2 CUPS JASMINE RICE

SALT

In a 3-quart saucepan bring 3¼ cups water to a boil. Add the tea bags, remove from the heat, and allow to steep for 15 minutes. Discard the tea bags and stir in the rice. Bring to a boil, reduce the heat to very low, cover, and cook for 15 minutes. Remove from the heat and set aside, covered, for 10 minutes.

Uncover, fluff with a fork, season lightly with salt, and transfer to a serving dish.

I have long been tempted to try simmering Asian jasmine rice in jasmine tea. I liked the idea of it and figured it might double-down on the alluring fragrance. I finally got around to it to accompany the Thai Red Seafood Curry (opposite), a dish that calls for rice to sop up the sauce. It was fragrant indeed. It is essential to let the rice sit for ten minutes before serving.

SERVES 10 TO 12

Steak à la Stone

THE PALM

MAMIE'S PEPPER HASH (RECIPE FOLLOWS)

¼ CUP EXTRA VIRGIN OLIVE OIL

3 CUPS WHOLE-GRAIN BREAD, CUT INTO ½-INCH CUBES

4 (12-OUNCE) BONELESS NEW YORK STRIP LOIN STEAKS,
    1½ INCHES THICK

SALT AND FRESHLY GROUND BLACK PEPPER

2 TABLESPOONS MINCED FLAT-LEAF PARSLEY LEAVES

Place the pepper hash in a bowl and allow to come to room temperature.

Heat the oil in a large heavy skillet over medium heat. Add the bread cubes and sauté, stirring, until they're lightly browned, about 3 minutes. Fold them into the pepper hash. Spread on a large serving platter.

Grill or broil the steaks to the desired degree of doneness, turning once. Set them aside to rest for 15 to 20 minutes. Season with salt and pepper.

To serve, cut the steaks on the bias in ½-inch-thick slices and arrange on the pepper hash. Shower with the parsley.

The Palm restaurants, now a nationwide chain, offer much the same menu everywhere. But none have the gracious, historic setting of the East Hampton branch in the old Huntting Inn. Among the popular menu classics is this steak dish involving slices of strip loin on a bed of peppers and onions on toast. But instead of sautéed onions and pimentos on toasted bread we're using a delicious pepper and onion relish with croutons, a recipe that came from an LVIS member.

SERVES 12

This chunky, sweet-and-sour relish keeps for weeks in the refrigerator, or can be processed in sterilized jars in a water bath for shelf-stable storage. Consider it alongside steaks, lamb chops, or chicken when you light the outdoor grill, or serve it with seafood or fish.

MAKES 4 CUPS

Mamie's Pepper Hash
REBECCA DISUNNO

2 LARGE RED BELL PEPPERS

2 LARGE GREEN BELL PEPPERS

1 LARGE SWEET ONION, COARSELY CHOPPED

¾ CUP APPLE CIDER VINEGAR

2 TABLESPOONS SUGAR

1 TEASPOON SALT

1 TEASPOON CELERY SEEDS

Core the peppers, removing the fleshy ribs. Cut into pieces. Place the peppers and onion in a food processor and pulse until chopped into ¼-inch pieces. Transfer the vegetables to a 3-quart pot, draining any juices.

Bring 4 cups of water to a boil in a separate pot or kettle. Pour over the vegetables and let sit for 15 minutes. Drain well. Return the vegetables to the pot.

Add the vinegar, sugar, salt, and celery seeds. Bring to a simmer over medium-low heat and cook for 15 minutes, stirring once or twice. Watch the heat carefully so all the vinegar does not cook off. Transfer to a container and refrigerate, or pack in sterilized jars and seal for later use.

Apricot Pecan Bars
NANCY PEARSON

4 OUNCES (1 STICK) UNSALTED BUTTER, SOFTENED

⅔ CUP DRIED APRICOTS, FINELY CHOPPED

¼ CUP GRANULATED SUGAR

1⅓ CUPS SIFTED ALL-PURPOSE FLOUR

½ TEASPOON BAKING POWDER

¼ TEASPOON SALT

2 LARGE EGGS, LIGHTLY BEATEN

1 CUP PACKED LIGHT BROWN SUGAR

½ TEASPOON VANILLA EXTRACT

1 CUP CHOPPED PECANS

CONFECTIONERS' SUGAR

Preheat the oven to 350°F. Use a little of the butter to lightly grease a 9 by 13-inch glass baking dish.

Place the apricots in a small saucepan, add water to cover by 1 inch, and bring to a boil. Reduce the heat to low and simmer for 10 minutes. Remove from the heat and drain well.

Place the granulated sugar and 1 cup of the flour in a food processor or a bowl. Pulse or mix to combine. Add the butter and pulse or mix with a fork until the mixture is crumbly. Spread the mixture evenly in the baking dish, pressing down on it. Bake for about 25 minutes, until lightly browned.

Meanwhile, whisk together the remaining ⅓ cup flour, the baking powder, and salt in a small bowl. In a separate bowl, beat the eggs until slightly frothy. Gradually beat in the brown sugar. Add the flour mixture and combine well. Stir in the vanilla, pecans, and apricots. Spread the mixture over the baked layer and return to the oven. Bake for about 30 minutes, until the top is browned and slightly springy to the touch. Remove from the oven and let cool completely. Sift confectioners' sugar over the top and cut into 2-inch squares.

IMPROVEMENT: If you're tempted to embellish these with chocolate glaze (page 109), who would complain?

This is a family recipe from an LVIS member who recalls receiving packages of the bars when she was in college and not wanting to share them with the rest of the dorm. They're easily made.

MAKES 24 BARS

This is a family recipe from the winemaker and partner in the South Fork's premier winery, Wölffer Estate in Sagaponack. Roth said it's his sister's recipe and insists that it not be varied. Still, with all those egg whites, it seemed to beg to include a few yolks, which add richness to the cake. Serve it with red wine, maybe a Wölffer merlot.

SERVES 10 TO 12

Red Wine Cake (Rotweinkuchen)
ROMAN ROTH, WÖLFFER ESTATE

10½ OUNCES (2 STICKS PLUS 5 TABLESPOONS) UNSALTED BUTTER, SOFTENED

1 CUP FINELY GROUND ALMONDS

2 CUPS ALL-PURPOSE FLOUR

2 TEASPOONS BAKING POWDER

1½ TEASPOONS GROUND CINNAMON

1½ CUPS GRANULATED SUGAR

3 LARGE EGG YOLKS

¼ TEASPOON VANILLA EXTRACT

6 OUNCES BITTERSWEET CHOCOLATE, COARSELY GRATED

5 OUNCES (⅔ CUP) RED WINE

6 LARGE EGG WHITES

CONFECTIONERS' SUGAR

Preheat the oven to 350°F. Use a little of the butter to grease a 10-inch Bundt pan or other ring mold.

In a small bowl, whisk together the almonds, flour, baking powder, and cinnamon.

Using an electric mixer, beat the remaining butter and gradually add the granulated sugar. Continue beating until pale and light, at least 5 minutes. Beat in the egg yolks one at a time, then beat in the vanilla. Fold in the flour mixture, then the chocolate. Stir in the red wine. In a separate clean mixer bowl, beat the egg whites until they hold peaks but are still creamy. Fold them in.

Pour the batter into the prepared pan and bake for about 1 hour, until a cake tester comes out clean. Allow to cool completely, remove from the pan, and sift confectioners' sugar over the cake before serving.

CHOWDER SUPPER

Making a steaming bowl of hearty soup, thick
with bivalves and vegetables, the centerpiece for
a dinner is not unusual in these parts. It's an
off-season delight. And a menu that begins with
Peconic Bay scallops must be off-season, since
the scallops are a fall and winter specialty.
From the ingredients in the various recipes to the
contributors, this menu has East Hampton written
all over it. Glasses should be filled with beer or
a simple sauvignon blanc.

Peconic Bay Scallops Oreganata • Old Bonac Clam Chowder
Stir-Fried Broccoli Stems • Orange Pudding

Peconic Bay Scallops Oreganata

MICHAEL ROZZI, THE 1770 HOUSE

2 POUNDS FRESH PECONIC BAY SCALLOPS, SIDE TENDONS REMOVED

2 TABLESPOONS EXTRA VIRGIN OLIVE OIL

⅓ CUP PANKO BREAD CRUMBS

1½ TEASPOONS GRATED LEMON ZEST

4 TEASPOONS CHOPPED FRESH OREGANO OR MARJORAM LEAVES

1 TEASPOON FRESH THYME LEAVES

PINCH OF PAPRIKA

SALT AND FRESHLY GROUND BLACK PEPPER

1 CLOVE GARLIC, CRUSHED AND MINCED

3 TABLESPOONS LEMON JUICE

3 TABLESPOONS DRY WHITE WINE

5 TABLESPOONS UNSALTED BUTTER, CUT INTO PATS

Toss the scallops with 1½ teaspoons of the olive oil in a large bowl.

Place the bread crumbs in a small, heavy skillet and toast over medium heat, stirring often, until lightly browned, 4 to 5 minutes. Remove from the heat and mix in the lemon zest, 3 teaspoons of the oregano, the thyme, and paprika. Stir in 1½ teaspoons of the remaining olive oil and season with salt and pepper. Set aside.

Heat the remaining 1 tablespoon olive oil in a small skillet over medium-low heat. Add the garlic and cook until barely starting to brown. Add the lemon juice and wine and cook until reduced by half. Remove from the heat. Add the butter and the remaining 1 teaspoon oregano and let the butter melt, then whisk the sauce until smooth. Season with salt.

Heat a heavy skillet that can hold the scallops in a single layer over medium-high heat. Add the scallops to the pan and dust with salt and pepper. Turn them when they are lightly browned on one side, 3 to 4 minutes. Cook the scallops on the second side for about 2 minutes; remove from the heat. Pour in the lemon sauce.

Transfer the scallops and sauce to a shallow serving dish or individual ramekins, top with the seasoned bread crumbs, and serve.

The season of small, nut-sweet Peconic Bay scallops begins in early November and lasts, officially, through March, though weather conditions and demand can shut the door sooner. The best approach is to grab them when they're available because you never know. They're a peerless treasure, delicious nuggets to wreck the budget but a delight sautéed, baked, broiled, or even served raw, lightly dressed with citrus for ceviche. I like to bake them with parsley and garlic snail butter. Rozzi, the chef at the esteemed 1770 House in East Hampton, treats them with herbs, lemon, and garlic.

SERVES 6

IMPROVEMENT: It would not be a crime to serve these scallops over fettuccine or another pasta, enriched with a few splashes of heavy cream.

The painter and her husband, Jackson Pollock, were among the most celebrated of the East Hampton arts colony that also included names like Willem and Elaine de Kooning, Saul Steinberg, Robert Motherwell, and Adolph Gottlieb. Krasner and Pollock were passionate cooks. Krasner kept recipes on piles of note cards, most of which have been preserved. This one, from a file in the pantry of the Pollock-Krasner House, now a museum in Springs, was handwritten by Ms. Krasner. Its source remains a mystery.

SERVES 6

IMPROVEMENT: The orange slices can also be arranged in stemmed goblets. Add the custard and egg whites, garnish with the zest, and use a kitchen blowtorch to sear the top.

Orange Pudding
LEE KRASNER

3 NAVEL ORANGES
1½ TABLESPOONS COINTREAU (OPTIONAL)
3 TABLESPOONS CORNSTARCH
1½ CUPS WHOLE MILK
3 TABLESPOONS SUGAR
½ TEASPOON SALT
3 LARGE EGGS, SEPARATED
1 TEASPOON VANILLA EXTRACT

Grate 1 tablespoon zest from the oranges and set aside. Peel the oranges, removing all the white pith. Slice the oranges horizontally ¼ inch thick, remove any seeds, and arrange them, slightly overlapping, in a 4-cup baking dish. Alternatively, the dessert can be made in six individual baking ramekins, each with a 6-ounce capacity. Drizzle the oranges with the Cointreau, if using.

Place the cornstarch in a small bowl. Gradually add 3 tablespoons of the milk and mix until smooth. Place the remaining milk in a small, heavy saucepan, preferably nonstick. Whisk in the cornstarch mixture, 2 tablespoons of the sugar, the salt, and 2 teaspoons of the orange zest. Bring to a simmer over medium-low heat and cook, whisking, until the mixture thickens, about 5 minutes. Remove from the heat. Beat the egg yolks in another small bowl. Whisk in a few tablespoons of the milk mixture to temper the eggs, then whisk the egg yolks back into the saucepan. Add the vanilla. Bring just to a simmer and remove from the heat. Spoon over the oranges in the baking dish or dishes.

Set the broiler rack about 8 inches below the heat source and preheat the broiler. Beat the egg whites until frothy. Sprinkle with the remaining 1 tablespoon sugar and continue beating until stiff but still creamy. Spoon the egg whites onto the top of the contents in the baking dish or dishes. Strew with the remaining 1 teaspoon orange zest.

Place under the broiler and broil until the meringue topping is nicely browned, about 2 minutes, but watch carefully—it can go fast! Remove from the broiler, let cool for about 10 minutes, then serve.

FEAST *by the* FIRE

When the winter storms whip the whitecaps, East Hampton retreats indoors, the firewood stacked and ready. This supper for four, relying on many local ingredients, is a logistical breeze. Here's how it goes: the first-course clams can be broiled in advance and set aside. Then the chicken will go into the oven at 450°F, and when it comes out, the clams will follow to reheat for five minutes along with the cauliflower. Serve the clams while the cauliflower is roasting. When the guests have finished their clams, you can shut off the oven, leaving the cauliflower in it, and prepare the sauce for the chicken. Once the main course has been served and enjoyed, it's time to tackle the bananas. During your absence from the table to prepare the bananas you might consider serving some local cheeses (see page 172) to enjoy with one of the region's lovely white wines, a pinot blanc or chenin blanc perhaps.

Baked Clams • Roast Chicken with Tarragon
Roasted Cauliflower with Garlic and Rosemary • Bananas Foster

Baked Clams

LAWRENCE WALLACE, INLET SEAFOOD RESTAURANT

10 CHERRYSTONE CLAMS, WELL SCRUBBED

⅔ CUP DRY WHITE WINE

3 STRIPS BACON, PREFERABLY APPLEWOOD SMOKED

1 SMALL SHALLOT, MINCED

1½ TEASPOONS FINELY MINCED FRESH FLAT-LEAF PARSLEY LEAVES

1 TEASPOON MINCED FRESH THYME LEAVES

1 TEASPOON MINCED FRESH OREGANO LEAVES

2 TABLESPOONS UNSALTED BUTTER, MELTED

1½ TEASPOONS LEMON JUICE

1 CUP PLAIN PANKO BREAD CRUMBS

LEMON WEDGES FOR SERVING

Place the clams in a heavy 3-quart saucepan with ⅓ cup of the wine. Cover and cook over medium heat until the clams open, 8 to 10 minutes. Remove the clams to a bowl and set them aside until they are cool enough to handle. Strain the clam juice through a fine sieve and reserve.

Meanwhile, fry the bacon until lightly browned. Place on paper towels to drain. Add the shallot to the bacon fat and sauté over medium heat until the shallot is translucent, about two to three minutes. Add the remaining ⅓ cup wine, increase the heat to medium-high, and reduce the liquid until it just films the pan. Stir in the parsley, thyme, oregano, and reserved clam juice. Remove from the heat. Stir in the melted butter, lemon juice, and panko.

Shuck the clams, reserving 12 of the half-shells. Chop the clams and bacon together, preferably by hand. Fold the clams and bacon into the bread crumb mixture. Pack the mixture into the 12 half-shells. Cover and set aside until shortly before serving.

Preheat the broiler.

Line a baking sheet with foil and place the clams on it. Place under the broiler at a distance of about 6 inches and broil until the clams are nicely browned, about 3 minutes. Serve with lemon wedges.

Named according to size—from the smallest littlenecks to the next topnecks, then cherrystones, and finally quahogs or chowder clams, hard-shelled clams are a seaside pride and joy. Diggers, both commercial and amateur, regularly gather them to delight aficionados at raw bars, with pasta, in chowders and pies, and, like the ones in this recipe, baked in their shells. This dish comes from a restaurant that is run by Chef Larry Wallace and frequented by fishermen, baymen, and their families, and is about as far east, just shy of Montauk Point, as you can go.

SERVES 4

IMPROVEMENT: One of my proudest accomplishments has been mastering the art of opening clams (and oysters). The best way to learn is to watch a professional shucker who is willing to do it slowly for you to observe the technique; written instructions do not do the task justice. Use the humblest, plainest, least gimmicky clam knife you can buy.

Chef should be added to the resume of Dan Rizzie, an artist and musician who lives in Sag Harbor. This chicken with a delicious tarragon-mustard sauce calls for an unusual method for roasting and a professional technique for sauce making. For his chickens, Rizzie relies on Iacono Farm, an East Hampton institution (see page 188).

SERVES 4

IMPROVEMENT: If possible, use high-fat butter. The federal standard for butter is 80 percent fat, but there are butters sold that are anywhere from 82 to 85 percent fat. Those few percentage points mean there is less water in the butter, making it more effective for enriching and thickening sauces and for baking.

Roast Chicken with Tarragon
DAN RIZZIE

1 TABLESPOON KOSHER SALT OR FINE SEA SALT

½ TEASPOON FRESHLY GROUND BLACK PEPPER

1 (3- TO 4-POUND) CHICKEN, PREFERABLY LOCAL OR ORGANIC

1 TABLESPOON EXTRA VIRGIN OLIVE OIL

1 SHALLOT, MINCED

1 CUP CHICKEN STOCK

2 TEASPOONS DIJON MUSTARD

2 TABLESPOONS UNSALTED BUTTER, SOFTENED

1 TABLESPOON MINCED FRESH TARRAGON LEAVES

2 TEASPOONS LEMON JUICE

Place a 12-inch cast iron skillet in the oven. Heat the oven to 450°F.

Mix the salt and pepper together in a small bowl. Tie the legs of the chicken together and tuck the wingtips behind the chicken. Dry the chicken with paper towels. Rub the chicken all over with the olive oil. Reserve about ½ teaspoon of the salt and pepper mixture and rub the rest all over the chicken, inside and out.

Using oven mitts or a heavy folded towel, carefully place the chicken, breast-side up, in the hot skillet in the oven. Roast for 30 minutes. Turn off the oven and leave the chicken in the oven for another 30 minutes. Do not open the oven door during this time. At the end, an instant-read thermometer inserted in the breast should read 150°F, the thigh should register 165°F, and the skin should be nicely browned. Remove the pan from the oven and transfer the chicken to a cutting board. Place the pan on the stove. Have a warm serving platter ready.

Skim all but 1 tablespoon of the fat from the pan and discard it. Turn the burner to medium and add the shallot. Cook for a minute or two, until softened and starting to brown. Stir in the stock and mustard, scraping up any browned bits in the pan. Cook for a few minutes, until reduced to about ¾ cup. Remove the pan from the heat.

Cut the chicken into 8 or 10 sections and transfer to a warm platter. Tent with foil to keep warm. Return the skillet to a burner over very low heat. Whisk in the butter bit by bit. Stir in the tarragon and lemon juice. Season with some of the reserved salt and pepper if needed. Spoon the sauce over the chicken and serve.

Roasted Cauliflower with Garlic and Rosemary
LOIS NESBITT

1 HEAD CAULIFLOWER, WELL TRIMMED AND BROKEN INTO FLORETS

2 TABLESPOONS EXTRA VIRGIN OLIVE OIL

SALT

4 CLOVES GARLIC, COARSELY CHOPPED

LEAVES FROM 2 BRANCHES FRESH ROSEMARY

Preheat the oven to 450°F. Line a baking sheet with foil.

Place the cauliflower in a bowl, rub with the olive oil, and season with salt. Spread the florets on the baking sheet and strew with the garlic and rosemary. Roast for about 20 minutes, until the cauliflower is tender when pierced with a paring knife but not falling apart. Transfer to a serving dish.

IMPROVEMENT: This recipe works equally well when broccoli is substituted for the cauliflower, or a mixture of both is used.

An artist who specializes in collages and art installations, this East Hampton resident and LVIS member is also an accomplished cook. An artful rendition of this recipe can be achieved by using a kaleidoscope of cauliflowers in yellow, purple, white, and even green, all from local farm stands.

SERVES 4

Bananas Foster

MERCEDES RUEHL

2 TABLESPOONS UNSALTED BUTTER

2 TABLESPOONS DARK BROWN SUGAR

3 RIPE BUT FIRM BANANAS, PEELED AND HALVED LENGTHWISE

½ CUP DARK RUM

VANILLA ICE CREAM

Place the butter and brown sugar in a skillet large enough to hold the bananas in a single layer. Cook over medium-high heat until the butter is melted and caramelized with the sugar, 2 to 3 minutes. Remove from the heat. Place the bananas in a single layer in the pan and baste with the caramel. Place the rum in a small saucepan.

Heat the bananas for a couple of minutes, basting them occasionally and turning them once, until they are warmed through. Remove from the heat and, if drama is your thing, bring the skillet to the dining table, placing it on a trivet. Heat the rum until it's starting to simmer. Quickly bring the rum to the table and pour it over the bananas. Stand back and, using a long fireplace match, ignite the rum. When the flames subside, quarter the bananas and serve with their sauce and scoops of ice cream. If showmanship makes you nervous, you can accomplish all of this in the privacy of your kitchen (where you should have a fire extinguisher).

IMPROVEMENT: When the season's bounty includes luscious fruit, Ruehl suggests substituting quartered ripe peaches for bananas.

The Academy Award– and Tony Award–winning actress is an East Hamptonite who might cross your path at antiques shows and in food markets. And of course she's all about drama, of which there is plenty in this crowd-pleasing dessert. Cue the applause.

SERVES 4

Acknowledgments

The Cookbook Committee is forever grateful to Florence Fabricant, whose exquisite way with food and words has taken the LVIS's thirteenth cookbook to heights we could not have achieved without her.

For all his extra miles on our behalf, we thank Doug Young, whose magical photographs evoke all the beauty and history of our beloved East Hampton.

We acknowledge the late Cameron Prather for his brilliant contributions to our food and tabletop styling. We are deeply grateful to executive chef Michael Rozzi of The 1770 House for coming onboard to help complete the book as our food stylist and recipe preparer. And thanks to Carol Covell and all at The 1770 House for allowing us to photograph many of the recipes at the inn and restaurant.

For graciously opening their beautiful homes and gardens to us, we thank Belinda and Rick Gilbert and Mary Jane and Charles Brock. Other wonderful location shoots were provided by the Falkowski Farm, Amber Waves Farm, Pike Farms, Balsam Farms, The Milk Pail, MariLee's Farm Stand, Sag Harbor Florist, Mill House Inn, Home Sweet Home Museum, the Breakers MTK, Devon Yacht Club, Quail Hill Farm, Fairview Farm at Mecox, and Channing Daughters Winery.

Meg Huylo's tabletop styling is evident throughout the book as are beautiful flower arrangements by Missi Bullock of Missi Flowers.

For providing prepared food and tabletop props, we thank Amy Acierno of Miss Amy's Preserves, chef Joe Realmuto, chef Carolyn Stec, chef Jason Weiner, Carissa's the Bakery, Jennifer Mulligan, The Seafood Shop, Mecox Dairy, Wölffer Estate, Citarella, Claws Seafood, Giunta's Meat Farms, Jennifer Georges, Linda Ringhouse, Clic Home East Hampton for loaning many beautiful tabletop accessories used throughout the book, Thayer's Hardware and Patio, Edtoba, The Interior, Anna Clejan, and Marders. A very special thanks to the Shops at LVIS for their endless generosity.

The historical photographs that add such richness to our book were thoroughly researched and generously provided by *The East Hampton Star*.

—LVIS

I was extremely pleased and flattered that the Cookbook Committee for LVIS reached out to me to write their landmark 125th anniversary cookbook. I had been collecting LVIS cookbooks over the years and was always interested in and charmed by them. For this one, LVIS was on the front lines. Digging deep into the collection of new recipes received from a diverse cross-section of East Hampton's cooks, both amateur and professional, as well as selecting many winners from past books, took the best part of a rewarding year. It was a task that could not have been accomplished without the tireless assistance of the committee members, Mary Talley, Bess Rattray, Barbara Lambert, Bonny Reiff-Smith, Afton DiSunno, and, all too briefly, Bonnie Krupinski, led by Anne Thomas, the indomitable former president of LVIS. They were there to help shape the book, to scour the files of LVIS for information, and to step in to test a number of the recipes.

To bring the book to life I want to thank Doug Young, our photographer, for his exquisite work, and the stylists Michael Rozzi and the late Cameron Prather. My daughter, Patricia Fabricant, the book's designer with whom I adore working (this is our sixth cookbook together), deserves to take a bow. At Rizzoli USA our thanks go to Charles Miers, the visionary, demanding yet genial publisher who made this book possible. Also, Aliza Fogelson, the editor, and her team at Rizzoli, including Kaija Markoe, the production manager, and Leda Scheintaub, the copy editor, provided essential guidance and did a masterful job of wrestling the manuscript to the ground together; they were our safety net and for that we are so grateful.

—FLORENCE FABRICANT

LVIS Cookbook Committee

Ruth Appelhof

Afton DiSunno

Bonnie Bistrian Krupinski (In Memoriam)

Barbara Lambert

Bess Rattray

Bonny Reiff-Smith

Mary Talley

Anne P. Thomas

The Ladies' Village Improvement Society Cookbook is made possible, in part, by a generous contribution from Anne Perkerson Thomas in honor of her sister, Carol Perkerson Foster (1950–2019).

ARCHIVAL PHOTOGRAPHY CREDITS

The archival photographs on pages 2–3, 6–7, 16–25, and 92–93 come from the collection of *The East Hampton Star*.

First published in the
United States of America in 2020 by
Rizzoli International Publications, Inc.
300 Park Avenue South, New York, NY 10010
www.rizzoliusa.com

Copyright © 2020 Florence Fabricant and
The Ladies' Village Improvement Society of
East Hampton, Long Island, New York, Inc.
Foreword: Martha Stewart
Photography: Doug Young
Additional photography credits appear on page 247.

The recipe on page 30 was used with permission from
Pierre Franey's Cooking in America (Alfred A. Knopf, 1994).

The recipes on pages 59, 78, 126, 129, 142, 163, 200, 206, 221,
and 231 were adapted from *The East Hampton LVIS Centennial
Cookbook* (Wimmer, 1994).

The recipe on pages 112–113 was used with permission from
A French Chef Cooks at Home by Jacques Pépin (Touchstone, 1980).

The recipes on pages 132–133 were used with permission from
*The Living Clearly Method: 5 Principles for a Fit Body, Healthy Mind &
Joyful Life* by Hilaria Baldwin (Rodale Press, 2016).

The recipe on page 205 was used with permission from *Make It Ahead: A
Barefoot Contessa Cookbook*. Copyright © 2012 by Ina Garten. Published
by Clarkson Potter/Publishers, an imprint of Random House, LLC.

Publisher: Charles Miers
Editor: Aliza Fogelson
Design: Patricia Fabricant
Production Manager: Kaija Markoe
Managing Editor: Lynn Scrabis

*Pages 2–3: A snowy egret
in Town Pond, which was
transformed from a swamp to a
postcard view by the LVIS early
in the twentieth century.*

*Pages 6–7: Members of the
Social Register gathered with
the LVIS for a "Society Street
Fair" in the late 1920s.*

*Page 8: A lush view at Grey
Gardens, the town's most
famous, and quintessential,
summer house by the beach.*

*Page 242: Mulford Farm, at
the heart of the East Hampton
Village historic district that was
spurred into existence by
the LVIS's Landmarks
Committee in the 1970s.*

Printed in China

2020 2021 2022 2023 / 10 9 8 7 6 5 4 3 2 1

ISBN: 978-0-8478-6519-2
Library of Congress Control Number: 2019953032

Visit us online:
Facebook.com/RizzoliNewYork
Twitter: @Rizzoli_Books
Instagram.com/RizzoliBooks
Pinterest.com/RizzoliBooks
Youtube.com/user/RizzoliNY
Issuu.com/Rizzoli

First published in the
United States of America in 2020 by
Rizzoli International Publications, Inc.
300 Park Avenue South, New York, NY 10010
www.rizzoliusa.com

Copyright © 2020 Florence Fabricant and
The Ladies' Village Improvement Society of
East Hampton, Long Island, New York, Inc.
Foreword: Martha Stewart
Photography: Doug Young
Additional photography credits appear on page 247.

The recipe on page 30 was used with permission from
Pierre Franey's Cooking in America (Alfred A. Knopf, 1994).

The recipes on pages 59, 78, 126, 129, 142, 163, 200, 206, 221,
and 231 were adapted from The East Hampton LVIS Centennial
Cookbook (Wimmer, 1994).

The recipe on pages 112–113 was used with permission from
A French Chef Cooks at Home by Jacques Pépin (Touchstone, 1980).

The recipes on pages 132–133 were used with permission from
The Living Clearly Method: 5 Principles for a Fit Body, Healthy Mind &
Joyful Life by Hilaria Baldwin (Rodale Press, 2016).

The recipe on page 205 was used with permission from Make It Ahead: A
Barefoot Contessa Cookbook. Copyright © 2012 by Ina Garten. Published
by Clarkson Potter/Publishers, an imprint of Random House, LLC.

Publisher: Charles Miers
Editor: Aliza Fogelson
Design: Patricia Fabricant
Production Manager: Kaija Markoe
Managing Editor: Lynn Scrabis

Printed in China

2020 2021 2022 2023 / 10 9 8 7 6 5 4 3 2 1

ISBN: 978-0-8478-6519-2
Library of Congress Control Number: 2019953032

Visit us online:
Facebook.com/RizzoliNewYork
Twitter: @Rizzoli_Books
Instagram.com/RizzoliBooks
Pinterest.com/RizzoliBooks
Youtube.com/user/RizzoliNY
Issuu.com/Rizzoli

*Pages 2–3: A snowy egret
in Town Pond, which was
transformed from a swamp to a
postcard view by the LVIS early
in the twentieth century.*

*Pages 6–7: Members of the
Social Register gathered with
the LVIS for a "Society Street
Fair" in the late 1920s.*

*Page 8: A lush view at Grey
Gardens, the town's most
famous, and quintessential,
summer house by the beach.*

*Page 242: Mulford Farm, at
the heart of the East Hampton
Village historic district that was
spurred into existence by
the LVIS's Landmarks
Committee in the 1970s.*